Shining Through the Psalms

A 150-Day Devotional Journey

Deborah Presnell

GRACE
PUBLISHING

BROKEN ARROW, OK

With love, I dedicate this book to
my husband, Alan.
Thank you for your patience while
listening to me read my devotions aloud.
Your feedback was insightful.
Your encouragement was good.
But your confidence in me and your love
top anything I've ever experienced.
Thank you for your faithfulness and
perseverance to journey with me
while I wrote this book.

How to Use This Book

By systematically reading the psalms and their accompanying devotion, you'll receive practical application for daily living.

Each devotion is divided into four parts:

Reading the selected psalm

Reading the devotion

Making personal application

Giving praises and thanksgiving to God

To read **the selected psalm** use a Bible version you're comfortable with and easily understand. There are many on the market from which to choose. In this book, all Scripture is taken from the *New American Standard Bible* (NASB) unless otherwise noted. Most often, the noted Scriptures will be from the ESV, NIV, NKJV, and NLT.

Prior to reading the psalm, pray and ask God to guide your thoughts. Ask God to reveal Himself to you and to provide insight and understanding. Ask Him to open your eyes to see what He wants you to see. After the devotion, talk openly with God about what you read, how you feel, what was confusing, surprising, what you liked, or didn't like.

Be honest with God. He already knows your thoughts. *Our awesome God bends low and inclines His ear to listen.*

I encourage you to read the additional scriptures and references in the **Read the devotion** section. There's no substitute for reading God's words for yourself. Underline special verses.

Write them on paper, index cards, and sticky notes. Write them on your heart.

Make It Personal is the section where you consider what the psalm and the devotion mean to you personally. Reflect on how they apply to your daily life. The Bible gives directions on how to live. Personal application is the beginning step to a victorious life. Embrace it.

Praise and thanksgiving are a focal point throughout the book of Psalms. This section offers you the opportunity to praise and thank God for what He is doing in your life. Praising God and thanking Him are similar, yet, they carry significant differences in their meaning and application. Both bring glory to God.

Praise is the act of complimenting God for who He truly is — His attributes and excellence. We praise God for what He has done for all people, apart from what He has done for us personally. Praise is acknowledging His perfections and admiring God. As we gain insight into God's character, praise flows more freely.

Thanksgiving is expressing appreciation for what God has done for us — His specific gifts and the blessings He has lavished on us and on others — past and present. Thanking God comes from a place of gratitude. It is the core of your thanksgiving.

There is a place at the end of each devotional to record your answers to Make It Personal, and Today I Bring Praise and Thanksgiving For.

Strong Roots

Read Psalm 1

Key Verse: 1:3 *He will be like a tree freely planted by streams of water, which yields its fruit in its season and its leaf does not wither; and in whatever he does, he prospers.*

The woman who walks with God is like a tree whose roots are firmly established and stretch to the river to receive their nourishment. She entwines her roots around the Word of God and ponders His precious words, for she knows they give her life. And she delights in them. His Word is a powerful source of spiritual energy, and she draws her strength from these living waters.

When the storms of life come, she won't be whisked away, for her strong root system holds fast. When the season of drought descends on her, she will not wither. When it is time to prune her limbs, she may experience discomfort, but this trimming enables her to produce beautiful, sweet-smelling fruit in season (Galatians 5:22-23). She is able to achieve that which has eternal value.

Jeremiah 17:7–8 tells us, *Blessed is the man who trusts in the Lord and whose trust is the Lord. For he will be like a tree planted by the water, that extends its roots by a stream and will not fear when the heat comes; but its leaves will be green, and it will not be anxious in a year of drought nor cease to yield fruit.*

The ungodly woman is also like a tree. But her roots do not go deep or stretch to the river for nourishment. When the winds rage, she is devastated and blown away. She withers in the heat, unable to bear fruit. She is unstable in her ways and lives aimlessly without direction.

When we need strength and stamina, we can go to God and tell Him all about it. He will help us establish strong roots.

Make It Personal

In whom or what are your roots grounded?

Today I Bring Praise and Thanksgiving For

God Laughs

Read Psalm 2

Key Verse: 2:4 *He who sits in the heavens laughs, the Lord scoffs at them.*

This psalm reads like a contemporary national newspaper or magazine.

The psalmist says that nations had rebelled against God, each other, and the kings during the transition from one king to another. Hatred for certain groups of people had caused bitter divisions. Hatred toward God had resulted in an uprising. People were living as if God didn't exist.

Our key verse tells us that God scoffed at them. The Hebrew term for *scoff* is "galas." It means "to mock; an outward expression of superiority." God's tone is sarcastic: *You scheme, strategize, and devise plans to rule the world, and think you can steal My control?* God laughed at their foolish thinking and idiotic behavior. He laughed at their ridiculous belief that they were in charge.

And God is still laughing today.

Almighty God controls, manages, and commands the entire world. Those who mock God and resist His control will meet Him face to face when they die. They won't be mocking then. They'll bow before Him with fear and trembling.

Observing wicked behaviors in a society that appears to be overrun with God-haters and evil doers can generate a lot of anxiety. Does God see their sin?

People with immoral, depraved hearts believe they will escape because they assume they're in control. But those who practice evil — openly or secretly — believing that God does not see or care, are mistaken. God created the world and He controls it.

In Revelation 1:17 the apostle John wrote, *When I saw Him, I fell at His feet like a dead man. And He placed His right hand on me, saying, "Do not be afraid; I am the first and the last."*

Isaiah 45:6–7 tells us, *Men may know from the rising to the setting of the sun that there is no one besides Me. I am the Lord, and there is no other, the One forming light and creating darkness, causing well-being and creating calamity; I am the Lord who does all these.*

Be encouraged. Evil cannot win. God has all the power.

Make It Personal

What rebellious acts against God do you most often see within your community? What can you do to remember that God is in control?

Today I Bring Praise and Thanksgiving For

My Shield

Read Psalm 3

Key Verse: 3:3 *You, O Lord, are a shield about me.*

A soldier's shield had many uses. The various ways it could be used made it a crucial weapon in battle.

A scene in the movie *Risen* shows one example. Every soldier on the battlefield holds a shield in front of his body. In unison all the men lift their shields above their heads, transforming their shields into a protective covering for the entire army. Seconds later, the men at the back of the line climb onto the shields and run across them toward the front line.

To make a shield more lethal, a spike protruded from the front of some shields. Roman soldiers used their shields for breaching walls and for carrying wounded bodies off the battlefield. Shields were also used as protection from the sun and rain.

Greek soldiers used their shields to create a rectangular formation called a phalanx. This was considered to be the deadliest battle formation of the ancient world. Some shields had a metal piece across the middle, which enabled the soldier to use the shield as a weapon to punch the enemy or to push forward. The shield was also used for protection against fiery enemy arrows.

In the New Testament, Paul wrote about a shield. In Ephesians 6:16, he wrote about the shield of faith: *Taking up the shield of faith with which you will be able to extinguish all the flaming arrows of the evil one.*

Life is a battlefield. Our enemy, the devil, throws fiery darts of doubt, stress, betrayal, and worthlessness, attempting to sabotage our emotional and spiritual health. But God is our shield. He won't allow the devil's flaming arrows to pierce us.

Today we can be assured that God will help us with our defensive strategy.

Make It Personal

Which fiery dart is Satan hurling toward you today? In what ways do you need God to protect you with His shield?

Today I Bring Praise and Thanksgiving For

Set Apart

Read Psalm 4

Key Verse: 4:3 *Know that the Lord has set apart the godly man for Himself; the Lord hears when I call to Him.*

*I*n many ancient cultures, a king's package or letter was stamped with a seal to show its authenticity. If the package lacked the seal it was considered inauthentic. The royal seal on a package also indicated its great worth, because it belonged to the king.

When we choose to put our faith in Jesus Christ, we are set apart and marked as Children of God. Ephesians 1:13 tells us this: *When you heard the word of truth, the gospel of your salvation, and believed in Him, you were sealed with the promised Holy Spirit* (ESV). God sealed us with the Holy Spirit at the moment we believed. The verse's wording indicates much more than the Holy Spirit being given or lent to us. When a new believer is sealed by the Holy Spirit, she is owned by God; her eternity's security is guaranteed. God is the Highest King and we are authentically His.

We are no ordinary package. We belong to King Jesus. A footnote in the *New King James Version Thomas Nelson Study Bible* explains the significance of our new identity: "The godly enjoy special blessings because the Lord has set them apart."[1]

In Timothy 2:19 the apostle Paul tells us, *Nevertheless, the firm foundation of God stands, having this seal, "The Lord knows those* who are His," and, "Everyone who names the name of the Lord is to abstain from wickedness."

Because we bear God's seal, we're set apart to follow His commandments and obey His words. What follows are His blessings.

Imagine. We're placed in the royal family of the highest King and sealed with the Holy Spirit. Now that makes for a beautiful package.

Make It Personal

How would you describe the feeling of being set apart and stamped with a seal indicating you belong to God?

Today I Bring Praise and Thanksgiving For

Finding Favor

Read Psalm 5

Key Verse: 5:12 *It is You who blesses the righteous man, O Lord, You surround him with favor as with a shield.*

*T*he word *favor* can be defined as "approval, partiality, (and) support."

God's favor is portrayed throughout the Bible:

God granted Daniel favor and compassion in the sight of the commander of the officials (Daniel 1:9).

The boy Samuel was growing in stature and in favor both with the Lord and with men (1 Samuel 2:26).

The angel said to her, "Do not be afraid, Mary; for you have found favor with God (Luke 1:30).

David found favor in God's sight, and asked that he might find a dwelling place for the God of Jacob (Acts 7:46).

Noah found favor in the eyes of the Lord (Genesis 6:8).

God did not say these were His favorite people, only that He showered favor on them. All five-people had something in common. In their confusion and imperfection, they humbly sought the Lord and obeyed Him.

God's favor is still poured out on us today. Do you secretly wonder if God favors others more than you? Isaiah 66:2 tells us, *To this one I will look, to him who is humble and contrite of spirit, and who trembles at My word.*

Who is "this one"? The one who sets aside independence and self-reliance and depends on God. The one who seeks to know Him better, by reading His Word. The one who chooses to obey His Word, even when it's difficult. The one who is remorseful for sin, but not frightened of the God who forgives.

God loves His children to come to Him as much as we love our children to come to us. Let's ask Him to help us recognize the favor He imparts.

Make It Personal

Do you find it difficult to believe that God favors you? Why or why not?

Today I Bring Praise and Thanksgiving For

Depression

Read Psalm 6

Key Verse: 6:6 *I am weary with my sighing; every night I make my bed swim, I dissolve my couch with tears.*

Who wrote such desperate statements?

These are the words of David. You know the one — the shepherd boy, who later slew the giant Goliath and eventually became King David, father to the wisest man known on earth — Solomon.

Many scholars believe this was one of the penitential psalms David wrote after his sin with Bathsheba. Therefore, this bout of depression would be the result of sin.

In complete transparency, David revealed his vulnerability and his human flaws. David was depressed. Maybe that's one reason we like him. We can relate to him, and in this way, we feel normal.

Maybe we feel miserable and disheartened. Emotionally, we've had enough. We're weary and resigned to the fact that the pressures are too much. We're exhausted from groaning and crying. Perhaps we're in a powerful leadership role. Still, we may be somewhat disillusioned. Life is hard and doesn't always turn out the way we expect.

David was open and real before God. He asked the hard questions. At least sixteen times in this psalm, David asked, "How long will the pain continue?" But what makes David stand out as much as his "realness" is his ability to end his rant by declaring that God had heard his prayer and would answer. His transparency with God coupled with his endless praise made David a strong leader, despite his depressed days.

We can be strong too, when we're not afraid to admit to God how we feel in the hidden places of our soul. We can be strong when we understand that depression doesn't define our abilities, indicate weakness, or that we'll be immobile forever. We're strong when we declare that we'll trust God by bringing acclamations of praise and thanksgiving while we wait.

Make It Personal

What, if anything, do you need to be real about with God? How can a Christ-follower's depression differ from a non-believer's depression?

Today I Bring Praise and Thanksgiving For

Lies and Schemes

Read Psalm 7

Key Verses: 7:1-2 *O Lord my God, in You I have taken refuge; save me from those who pursue me, and deliver me, or he will tear my soul like a lion.*

Fictional programs or reality TV shows, often have similar story lines. For example, one story line could go like this: A young, attractive woman begins her career working at a Fortune 500 company. She's efficient and professional and is well liked by others. But her competitive and jealous supervisor feels threatened. Without justifiable cause to fire the young woman, the superior spreads embellished truths and lies throughout the office. Many co-workers side with the supervisor for their own selfish reasons. The victim becomes excluded, often hiding in the bathroom to cry. Several pursue her with the intent to ruin her life. They want failure and demise for her and plot how to make this happen.

A similar story unfolded more than 2,000 years ago. Young David worked for King Saul. Everyone loved David and that made Saul angry. Saul's jealousy burned within him so much that he desired to kill David. Cush, in his desire to get in good with king Saul, lied to Saul about David. Now Saul was out to destroy David and Cush was laughing all the way.

Same ingredients for a fiasco — lies, schemes, jealousy, selfishness — more than 2,000 years apart.

Sometimes these realities can intertwine with ours.

Have you ever felt that some person was in pursuit of you? Maybe he or she inaccurately judged you and the behavior that followed was exclusion, snickers, gossip, and rolled eyes. They schemed amongst themselves to see you fail.

Overwhelmed with an anxiety-producing situation, you want to scream.

In tough situations like this we don't have to feel defeated. Rather, we can move into the strategic position for battle — the impactful position on our knees — and cry-out to God. That's what David did. He turned Saul and his scheming men over to the Lord.

God vindicated David. He will vindicate us too.

Make It Personal

When have you been wrongly accused or judged? How did you handle it? How did God vindicate you? What did God teach you from the situation?

Today I Bring Praise and Thanksgiving For

God's Perfect Wordless Book

Read Psalm 8

Key Verse: 8:3 *I consider Your heavens, the work of Your fingers, the moon and the stars, which You have ordained.*

Astronomers tell us that, depending on its mass, a star can shine for about ten billion years. David may have been gazing up at the twinkling stars while penning this psalm, which could mean we can look at the same stars that captured David's attention.

Ralph Waldo Emerson wrote, "If the stars came out only once in a century, people would stay up all night gazing at them."[3] Would you?

David looked at the stars and he worshipped Almighty God. When he pondered all of nature, he felt the presence of God. In verse nine, David called God *majestic* (NIV) and *excellent* (KJV).

God created the sun, moon, stars and galaxies. He scheduled the seasons and the ocean tides. He made every colorful bird, and every gorgeous field of flowers. He fashioned magnificent waterfalls, the highest mountains and the teeny-tiny bumble bee. He created everything we see — and everything we don't see.

World-famous biologist Edward O. Wilson claims, "There may be as many as 1.6 million species of fungi in the world today, 10,000 species of ants, 300,000 species of flowering plants, between 4,000 and 5,000 species of mammals, and approximately 10,000 species of birds."[4]

The world in its entirety points us to the character of God. He is beautiful, creative, colorful, and magnificent. The zebra has stripes. The leopard has spots. That's not only creative, but also fun. Looking at the puppy with a single black spot around his eye on a body of white fur just makes us smile with delight.

Creation — one big, beautiful, wordless book that teaches us who God is. And everyone can read this wordless book. Let's make time to worship God. For example, let's star gaze. Envision what it must have been like to fix your gaze on twinkling stars for the first time. Then, like David, cheer for creation and praise God for His powerful handiwork.

Make It Personal

Does God's magnificent and creative work astonish you? Do you tell Him that? If you don't, what's holding you back?

Today I Bring Praise and Thanksgiving For

Unexplainable Wonders

Read Psalm 9

Key Verse: 9:1 *I will give thanks to the Lord with all my heart; I will tell of all Your wonders.*

Throughout the Bible — in both the Old Testament and the New — we read about God's miraculous work.

God does wonderful things. Do you need something wonderful to happen? Something so unbelievable that's it's impossible to explain how it happened? We all want the "unexplainable" in our lives. Perhaps we wish for

- strength when we feel beat down and weary.
- more time when we feel we're running out.
- joy when we're in the midst of a painful situation.
- favor in the eyes of people in authority over us.
- mended relationships.
- healing.

Perhaps what you want or need right now would be considered "a miracle." In 1 Chronicles 17:20 we read, *O Lord, there is none like You, nor is there any God besides You.*

Because there's no god like our God, only He can do extraordinary wonders — miracles. Author and pastor Robert A. Cook used to say, "If you can explain what's going on, God didn't do it." That sums it up perfectly![5]

Coincidences are not part of God's plans. He orchestrates divine appointments — meetings that are inspired, led, and specifically ordered by God.

We cannot explain these appointments or the way in which God intervenes, but we have experienced God's astonishing work in our lives. Who better to interfere in our business? God knows the future. In fact, from the beginning of our lives, God already knows the ending.

God is willing to do His part — the unexplainable. We must be willing to do ours. To call out to God and ask for that miracle — that event not explainable by natural or scientific laws and therefore considered to be the work of a divine agent — God's miraculous wonders we can't justify or rationalize. Then we'll say, "That must be God at work, for there's no other explanation."

Make It Personal

Do you need a miracle in your life? What unexplainable thing do you need to be done by our powerful God?

Today I Bring Praise and Thanksgiving For

Approachable

Read Psalm 10

Key Verse: 10:1 *Why do You stand afar off, O Lord? Why do you hide Yourself in times of trouble?*

"Why? Why does it do that, Daddy?" With pure curiosity the child asks his father for an explanation. Unafraid, and confident. Fully trusting.

David's persistent questioning gives us insight into his relationship with God. He believed that he could approach God. Like a small child, he was unafraid, confident, fully trusting. And that level of trust enabled him to be transparent and open. He comfortably questioned — and ranted —like a child before his daddy.

When I was younger, approaching God was foreign to me. In my mind, more important people, mostly preachers and missionaries, were first in line to approach God. I was at the back, double-checking my list to be sure the content was worthy to be discussed with God.

I had a false perception of God. Hebrews 4:16 tells us, *Let us draw near with confidence to the throne of grace, so that we may receive mercy and find grace to help in time of need.*

With boldness we approach God's throne and accept that He will reach down and pull us close. He is Holy God and Sovereign — creator of the Universe. But because we're His adopted children, He is Father — creator of our lives and instiller of our personal passions. In this place, God lavishes His love on us, and provides the help we desperately need.

God accepts everyone who approaches Him. Then we unpack our heavy suitcase and give to Him everything we have stashed or hidden inside — all our fears, disappointment and the crippling anxieties that weigh us down. We share our untold secrets of shame and regret and our most private thoughts. We give Him our confusion, our mix-ups, and uncertainties. We surrender our pride and sinful habits.

There, at the glorious throne of Almighty God, we lay them down.

Make It Personal

Do you have a David-like confidence to approach God with everything? If yes, where does this confidence come from? If no, what keeps you from talking to God as your loving Father?

Today I Bring Praise and Thanksgiving For

Confusion Versus Clarity

Read Psalm 11

Key Verse: 11:1 *How can you say to my soul, "Flee as a bird to your mountain . . . ."*

*B*eing on the run wasn't new to David. He'd fled and hidden many times. However, something was different about this particular excursion. In this crisis, David's counselors advised him to "run to the hills!" David studied the situation. Then he replied, "How can you say, flee to the mountain?" He ignored their advice and remained at his post . . . and God protected him. David knew the value of having counselors. But he knew God, too, and it was his knowledge of God and assurance of God's working in this situation that enabled him to trust that he was making the right decision.

Confusion can be defined as a "state of uncertainty." Confusion is part of our human nature. But it's not part of God's. First Corinthians 14:33 tells us *God is not a God of confusion.* The opposite of confusion is confidence and order.

Have you ever experienced a time when you conveyed your thoughts to your friends and family but they had different responses? With so many different ideas swarming, it's no wonder confusion sets in. It's especially difficult when opposing advice comes from people you love and trust.

Once, I asked a group of friends to help me make a decision about an upcoming missions opportunity. But when they offered conflicting opinions, I became confused. Like David, I felt it wasn't a time when clarity came through other people. I finally had to disregard their views and seek only God's counsel. I prayed for clarity to know what to do.

The Apostle Paul wrote in Ephesians 1:17–18, *May [God] give to you a spirit of wisdom and of revelation in the knowledge of Him. I pray that the eyes of your heart may be enlightened, so that you will know what is the hope of His calling.*

When we need clarity, we can search Scripture, trust God that His will is done, and pray for discernment.

If peace is in our heart, we step out in faith.

If you're dealing with confusion, allow God to be your advisor. He will remove the confusion and make His plan clear.

Make It Personal

How have you applied God's truth to a confusing situation?

Today I Bring Praise and Thanksgiving For

Single-mindedness

Read Psalm 12

Key Verse: 12:2 *They speak falsehood to one another; with flattering lips and a double heart they speak.*

Have you ever known someone who behaves one way when she's with one group and another way when she's with another group? How about a person who tells others what they should do, yet ignores those convictions when she's confronted with the same issues? These deceivers speak from both sides of their mouth. They talk this way because their hearts are divided — not committed to what they believe or which way they're going. The battle is within themselves —between their love for God and their love for the world.

Known as the Proverbs of the New Testament, the Book of James addresses the subject of being double-minded head on. James was writing to the first-century Christians when he wrote, *Draw near to God and He will draw near to you. Cleanse your hands, you sinners; and purify your hearts you double-minded* (James 4:8).

The word *double-minded* comes from the Greek word *dipsuchos* and means "a person with two minds or souls." A double-minded person speaks from two mind-sets. When a person speaks from two different points of view, depending on the crowd she's with, she might sound confusing.

In James 3:10–12, the apostle wrote, *From the same mouth come both blessing and cursing. My brethren, these things ought not to be this way. Does a fountain send out from the same opening both fresh and bitter water? Can a fig tree, my brethren, produce olives, or a vine produce figs? Nor can salt water produce fresh.*

In the big picture, we demonstrate what is inside us — what we're really made of. Just as a water fountain cannot produce both fresh water and salt water, neither should we be living our lives with thoughts or beliefs that vary depending on the people with whom we associate.

The way we become single-minded and wholly devoted to God is to draw near to Him. Spend time with Him and read His Word. When we believe His words are true and right, God will change our minds to reflect what's on His.

Make It Personal

When do you most often find your mind-set taking a worldly perspective? What helps you be wholly devoted to God?

Today I Bring Praise and Thanksgiving For

When Emotions Lie

Read Psalm 13

Key Verse: 13:1 *How long, O Lord? Will You forget me forever? How long will You hide Your face from me?*

Emotions such as joy and love enrich our lives. But when hardship comes, emotions can deceive us. Have you ever thought that God has forgotten all about you, that He doesn't care?

In our key verse, David asked the questions we, ourselves, have often asked. In painful situations especially, conflicting emotions envelop us.

Emotions can be unstable. They trick us. They lie. They are guided by our circumstances and what our eyes perceive; they fluctuate with shifting situations.

But God's Word doesn't fluctuate or lie. Numbers 23:19 tells us, *God is not human, that He should lie, not a human being, that He should change his mind. Does He speak and then not act? Does He promise and not fulfill?*

Satan messes with our emotions, so we'll be discouraged. When this happens, we must resist the urge to depend on *how we feel*. Instead, we can choose to stand on the powerful words of God. For example:

- When it feels like God is far away, tell God how you feel, then say that you believe His words in Hebrews 13:5: *I will never desert you, nor will I ever forsake you.*

- When you feel like God doesn't listen, remember Psalm 66:19: *Certainly God has heard. He has given heed to the voice of my prayer.*

- When you feel like God doesn't care, cry out to Him and recall the words in Psalm 103:8: *The Lord is compassionate and gracious, slow to anger and abounding in lovingkindness.*

- When you don't feel loved, choose to stand on His word that says, *I have loved you with an everlasting love* (Jeremiah 31:3).

- Instead of dwelling on your fears, tell God that you trust Him when He says, *Fear not; I am with you* (Isaiah 41:10).

- When doubt fills your heart, ask God to help you believe. *"I do believe; help my unbelief"* (Mark 9:24 NASB).

When we replay God's truth in our minds, not only does it help bring our emotions into proper balance, but it also restores our joy.

Make It Personal

Which of the bulleted examples describe how you feel? If none of those, is there another?

Today I Bring Praise and Thanksgiving For

Practical Atheist

Read Psalm 14

Key Verse: 14:1 *The fool has said in his heart, "There is no God."*

More than likely, we know a fool. We may have even been one at some point in our life. To get on the same page, though, let's clarify the meaning of fool.

A *fool* is defined as a person who lacks judgment. Synonyms include a person who is misled, deceived, or a laughingstock. Let's go further. The *King James Version Dictionary* uses *fool* in a Christian context, defining it as a person "who follows his own inclinations, who prefers trifling and temporary pleasures to the service of God and eternal happiness."[6] Ouch.

Could we be behaving like the fool in our key verse? We believe in God, but do we live as if there's no God watching or waiting to be involved in our lives?

The definition continues as "a weak Christian; a godly person who has much remaining sin and unbelief." Ouch again.

The Hebrew word for fool, *"nabal,"* means a person who is morally deficient. Further evidence that the statement "there is no God" refers to people who live like there is no God. These fools lack social conscience and any concern for religion. Without knowledge of God or biblical guidelines, they are left to their own wicked ways. Bible teacher Warren Wiersbe uses the phrase "practical atheist" to describe people who ignore God.

Psalm 14:4 gives us another description for those who do not call on God: "workers of wickedness." These people are puffed up with arrogance, and their self-will prompts them to do things on their own. They push God away. Do you want to be classified as someone who won't call on God?

Here's the good news. We never need to feel that God is bored with hearing from us again or that He thinks we're too needy. Clearly, God wants us to call on Him. He wants to be involved in every aspect of our lives.

Let's not live as fools but wisely allow God to be part of our lives.

Make It Personal

In what ways do you sometimes live like a practical atheist?

Today I Bring Praise and Thanksgiving For

Blameless

Read Psalm 15

Key Verses: 15:1–2 *Lord, who may dwell in your sacred tent? Who may live on your holy mountain? The one whose walk is blameless* (NIV).

*D*uring the exodus, God told Moses and Israel to build a great tent. This tent would be the tabernacle where man would meet God. David asked the question, "Who may come into the sacred tent?" He was motivated by a deep desire to be in the presence of God. The word *dwell* in Hebrew means "presence." David was asking who can come before God's presence?

The answer to the question in our key verse is, a person who is blameless (NIV) or one who walks uprightly (NASB). Thankfully, blameless doesn't mean sinless, for no person who has ever lived is sinless, except Jesus.

Wiersbe, defines *blameless* as "having to do with soundness of character, integrity, and complete loyalty to God."[7] Specifically, what does a blameless person look like? Packed into Psalm 15's five short verses are these characteristics:

- walks — a continuous motion indicating a regular pattern — with integrity
- thinks on things that are righteous
- speaks truth and does not slander or bring another

person down; is careful about showing disappointment in others; offers encouragement.

- resists living shamelessly and doesn't associate with the wicked.

- fears the Lord by treating Him with awe and respect; honors others who do likewise; is compelled to obey and trust God.

- keeps promises even when it's difficult to do so.

- uses resources to help others.

Paul, the writer of Philippians, also shed some light on blamelessness when he wrote, *Do all things without grumbling or disputing; so that you will prove yourselves to be blameless and innocent, children of God above reproach in the midst of a crooked and perverse generation, among whom you appear as lights in the world* (Philippians 2:14–15).

Sound impossible? Here's another attribute: A blameless person humbly depends on God for help. That's right. We can ask God to show us how to live in a way that pleases Him and to give us the strength to do it.

Psalm 119:1 promises, *How blessed are those whose way is blameless, who walk in the law of the Lord.*

Make It Personal

How can you practice integrity at home? At work? In the community?

Today I Bring Praise and Thanksgiving For

Fix Your Eyes

Read Psalm 16

Key Verse: 16:8 *I will keep my eyes always on the Lord (NIV).*

More than thirty years ago, my husband and I went skiing. I was eager to learn, and he was confident in his ability to teach me. After arriving at the nearby ski resort, we got my skis and boots and headed to the beginner's slope so I could get comfortable being on skis. Soon though, we ventured over to the ski lift for a ride up the mountain. Evergreens lined the trail of white against the backdrop of a sparkling blue sky, and swift skiers down below made the experience look easy and enjoyable.

But the beauty went unnoticed the moment I slipped off the ski lift bottom first. My husband graciously lifted me up. I gazed down from the top of the mountain, which seemed to have no end. Terror welled up in my chest and tears blurred my vision. I was frozen with fear.

My husband skied backwards down the mountain holding my hands, slowly pulling me along. But my eyes focused on the surroundings. Watching the other accomplished skiers distracted me. They were fast, graceful, and talented. I felt silly, incapable, and hopeless.

Recently, I dreamed about the experience. Again, my husband was skiing backwards down the mountain, holding my hands. But this time my eyes were closed. I couldn't see the difficulty of the slope, or the other more skilled skiers. I focused

37

on the end result. We finished ahead of the other skiers.

The difference in the first and second trip down the slope was what I determined to focus upon.

Perhaps obstacles in your life appear to be like that mountain — overwhelming, steep, or unattainable — and your circumstances seem impossible. When looking at others' accomplishments, you're left feeling inadequate, like I felt during my experience on the ski slope. And feeling silly, incapable, and hopeless you've become frozen with fear.

Spiritually speaking, we can turn away from what is distracting and do what Hebrews 12:2 says: Fix our eyes on Jesus and focus on the end result.

Make It Personal

What distractions keep you from being fully able to fulfill your purpose? What are some practical ways you can focus your attention on God?

Today I Bring Praise and Thanksgiving For

The Apple of God's Eye

Read Psalm 17

Key Verse: 17:8 *Keep me as the apple of the eye; hide me in the shadow of Your wings.*

Stevie Wonder released a song many of us may recall, "You Are the Sunshine of My Life." Within the lyrics is the phrase, "You are the apple of my eye."

When someone uses that phrase to describe us, we should be delighted! The phrase means that person cherishes us.

But Stevie Wonder didn't coin the phrase. First used in the Old Testament in Deuteronomy 32:10, the expression was used by God to show He cares for His people. Scripture tells us, *He found him in a desert land and in the wasteland, a howling wilderness; He encircled him, He instructed him, He kept him as the apple of His eye* (NKJV).

Zechariah 2:8 tells us that "the apple of His eye" is a descriptive phrase used by God to describe His people.

The apple, or pupil, is considered the most delicate part of the eye. When we look into another person's eyes, we see our own reflection. Similarly, when God looks into our eyes, He sees His reflection. We're made in the image of Christ. Everything in creation shows how beautiful God is. Because we're made in His image, we're beautiful.

We're precious, cherished, and beloved.

God continues to love and guard us by instructing us how to live. He says in Proverbs 7:2, *Keep My commandments and live, and my teaching as the apple of your eye.*

Are God's teachings the apple of our eye? Do we cherish God's Word? Do we accept the protection God provides by living within biblical boundaries?

Let's strive to live by God's Word and make His Word the apple of our eye.

Make It Personal

How beloved and cherished do you feel? In what ways does God see Himself in you? Do you cherish God's Word?

Today I Bring Praise and Thanksgiving For

Like a Deer

Read Psalm 18

Key Verse: 18:33 *He makes my feet like hinds' feet, and sets me upon my high places.*

What is difficult for you to do?

- Move past a hurt
- Move with confidence into new territory
- Let go of past shame and guilt
- Clarify and focus goals
- Use time more effectively
- Make decisions for yourself or other people

You're in good company. We all experience difficult times and decisions in our lives.

In this psalm, we see that although David was a king, he depended on God for his strength — both physically and mentally. In our key verse, David depicted a deer to illustrate how the mighty power of God works in our lives. The hind (a female deer) is alert. Her feet are swift and agile, enabling her to move through precarious places. God makes us like that deer — vigilant and able to escape an enemy or run with passion and purpose. God enables our feet to move through difficult places to take us where He wants us to go. Although our circumstances may seem like a rocky mountainside, we maneuver through the hard times with resolve and hope.

When we're alert to God's moving in our lives and earnestly seek His help, God will empower us with what we need. We may feel like the wall is too high. People might shake their heads and say we'll never get through. We may feel that we're in a tight spot and that difficulties have overtaken us. We may question if we'll ever get off rocky ground.

We will. Verse 29 describes the abilities we have through and with God's power. The psalmist wrote, *By You I can run upon a troop; and by my God I can leap over a wall.*

When we emerge victorious, we'll say as David said in verse 1, *I love You, O Lord my strength.*

Make It Personal

What tight spot are you currently in? What is God showing you about maneuvering through rocky places?

Today I Bring Praise and Thanksgiving For

Run Your Course

Read Psalm 19

Key Verse: 19:5 *It rejoices as a strong man to run his course.*

hen my daughters were in high school participating on track and cross-country teams, I stood on the sidelines cheering. Later on, I joined them in evening practice jogs around the neighborhood. Eventually, my youngest daughter and I ran a half-marathon together. On that quiet, foggy morning, God strengthened my physical body and showed me what's required for running our spiritual courses.

Hebrews 12:1 tells us: *Let us also lay aside every encumbrance and the sin which so easily entangles us, and let us run with endurance the race that is set before us.*

How can we make it to the finish line?

- Train regularly. My training involved a daily commitment to exercise my muscles. Reading God's Word daily exercises our spiritual commitments.

- Throw off weight. One training spot was a dirt track around the circumference of a small lake. Collecting a small rock for each lap helped me keep track of the number of laps I'd completed. However, the rocks were bulky and distracting. A sinful habit or attitude can resemble rocks in our pockets, weighing us down. We must toss that weight into the lake of God's forgiveness.

- Identify the real enemy. During my race, and with eyes downcast, I spotted a dead snake. Crushed. Unable to hiss. Powerless to strike. With God's Word and God-confident strength, we identify and fight Satan's attacks. He is powerless to strike; he cannot spread his venom.

- Live in community. My daughter was my support. Likewise, we need Christian friends. Find that friend. *Be that friend.*

- Persevere to the end. My race was long and hard. I wanted to quit. When we're on the hill of hardship and the wind has been knocked out of us, remember, with God, the hill will eventually level. We'll finish life's marathon stronger, with a sense of renewal and gratitude.

- Focus on the prize. A burst of energy allowed me to complete the race by sprinting across the finish line. One day our race will end and we'll run into the arms of Jesus. Philippians 3:14 tells us, *Press on toward the goal for the prize of the upward call of God in Christ Jesus.*

Look forward to the prize of hearing the Lord say, "Well done, good and faithful servant."

Make It Personal

How would your life look different if you applied Hebrews 12:1?

Today I Bring Praise and Thanksgiving For_

The Desires of Your Heart

Read Psalm 20

Key Verse: 20:4 *May He grant you according to your heart's desire, and fulfill all your purpose* (NKJV).

One afternoon I was caught off guard when an unexpected and surprising thought changed the trajectory of my life. An unforeseen passion — one I had never entertained — bubbled up inside me.

Where do thoughts like that come from?

Heartfelt desires burn in all of us. We have hopes and aspirations, whether it's for prayers to be answered, guidance for our lives, or provision for our happiness. God cares about our innermost desires and wants to shape them into what is truly best. The question is: Will we trust Him with these desires?

Author and Bible teacher John Piper wrote: "When God gives us our desires, He will not be contradicting His own supreme value in our lives as our supreme delight."[8] Piper compares this to what Jesus told us in John 15:7: *If you abide in me, and my words abide in you, ask whatever you wish, and it will be done for you."* The key to receiving our desires is to seek God with all our hearts and to want to obey Him.

Ultimately, God wants something greater for us than temporary happiness or success. He wants us to have a godly character and a heart like His. When we ask God to change our hearts and desires to align with His we're in agreement with Him, and He can grant our petition. And as He does, we take steps that lead us to our ultimate purpose.

On that sunny afternoon, God answered my prayer. I'd been asking God to align my thoughts with His. Truly, He planted within me the passion that led me to discover His will for that time. We can trust Him because what He wants for us is far better than what we could imagine for ourselves.

Make It Personal

What are your heart's desires? How will you apply God's word so that your desires align with His?

Today I Bring Praise and Thanksgiving For

What's Your Trigger?

Read Psalm 21

Key Verse: 21:2 *You have given him his heart's desire, and You have not withheld the request of his lips.*

Sometimes things happen and we don't understand their significance until much later. At other times, we pray specifically and God acts immediately. Either way, hindsight is 20/20 and beautiful — to clearly make the connection between an event and the hand of God.

Psalm 21 is a reflection of a victorious battle. Perhaps the victors were shocked by what God accomplished. Maybe they were giddy — couldn't stop laughing — for they were filled to the brim with joy. God answered their prayers and showed up with a bucket full — no, a well full — of strength. He showed His one-of-a-kind power and the victors were astounded.

Their response? All the joy, power, and victory triggered glad praises to God for His mighty work in their lives (Psalm 21:13).

Do we have a trigger? Or are we too busy to make connections between what happens in our lives and God's hand in it?

Today, make that connection. When have you witnessed God's power? When did you experience His favor? When did something that you feared would bring terrible destruction *not* happen? How much worse might things be without God's intervention? Can we ever know what He's saved us from?

Find some quiet time and reflect on the following questions.

Let the questions and your answers trigger spontaneous praise for the way God has dealt with you:

- When He gave you your heart's desire and answered your requests
- When He kept you from harm and destruction that you have yet to fully understand
- When He answered your prayer with "no" to protect you

Make It Personal

How would you explain praising God to a child?

Today I Bring Praise and Thanksgiving For

The Answer Is Yes!

Read Psalm 22

Key Verses: 22:16-18 *Dogs have surrounded me; a band of evildoers has encompassed me; they pierced my hands and my feet. I can count all my bones. They look, they stare at me; they divide my garments among them, and for my clothing they cast lots.*

*D*oes Jesus continue to love us despite our rebellious past or current sinful situation?

This psalm is one of many passages that prophesied the death of Jesus, God's Son. God knew from the beginning of time that Jesus was the only perfect, spotless sacrifice that could bear the sins of an entire world. God established every detail in the events leading up to His Son's death. Jesus came into the world as a baby, lived thirty-three years, and then died an agonizing death on a rugged cross that He Himself carried. No detail was left incomplete.

Jesus gave His life freely because He loved us so much. But His death not only paid our sin debt; it also enables us to have fellowship with Him forever. First Peter 3:18 tells us *Christ also died for sins once for all, the just for the unjust, so that He might bring us to God, having been put to death in the flesh, but made alive in the spirit.*

If we think Jesus has forsaken or forgotten us, we are sorely mistaken. Jesus didn't endure torment on the cross for our sakes to disregard us now. What would be the point? To suffer and then forget about the ones He suffered for? When Jesus gave His life, it was so that we could live forever and enjoy fellowship together.

Jesus loves us today as much as He did that dark afternoon when He took our sin on Himself. He cares about the problems we face. He understands the seemingly little details that change outcomes, and He wants to be an active participant in our lives.

Yes, Jesus still loves us.

Make It Personal

Think about the cross and what that event meant then. How does the cross affect you today?

Today I Bring Praise and Thanksgiving For

My Shepherd

Read Psalm 23

Key Verse: 23:1 *The Lord is my shepherd, I shall not want.*

o an Internet search about sheep, and you'll learn that sheep are among the world's most popular livestock. They're known for their tendency to follow other sheep. They're comfortable with their flock but are easily spooked when approached by humans. Compared to goats, sheep are less independent, less intelligent, more indecisive, and much more directionless. A series of experiments showed that if there's a hole in the ground, sheep will fall into it.

But recent research has shown that sheep are smarter than the dim-witted creatures we may have once thought they were. Sheep are smart enough to respond when called by name and they know and willingly follow their shepherd's voice.

If a sheep loses his way, the shepherd uses his rod and staff to discipline and direct. The shepherd will lovingly rescue his fallen one, should it fall in a hole.

In John 10:14 Jesus identifies Himself as the Good Shepherd. He then says, *"My sheep hear My voice, and I know them, and they follow Me"* (verse 27).

Just as the sheep know their names and come when called, Jesus calls us by name. Will we be as smart as sheep?

Jesus, our shepherd, promises to be with us through all seasons of life — the good and the bad. When we feel oppression, affliction, adversity, and pain, He draws us close. When we fall into a hole, He rescues us.

David, a former shepherd, was familiar with a shepherd's responsibilities and duties. He understood the powerful ways the shepherd uses his staff and rod and the effects these tools would have on the sheep's life.

We have a compassionate shepherd who left the ninety-nine to come after us. David chose to make God his personal Shepherd. Will we be as wise as David . . . and sheep?

Make It Personal

Is Jesus your shepherd? How have you experienced His tender care recently? What about His rod of discipline?

Today I Bring Praise and Thanksgiving For

A Pure Heart

Read Psalm 24

Key Verses: 24: 3–4 *Who may ascend into the hill of the Lord? And who may stand in His holy place? He who has clean hands and a pure heart.*

The Pharisees were the prominent Jewish religious leaders. The Scribes were the lawyers and teachers of the law, professional scholars who handed down legal decisions. The Gospels frequently grouped the two together.

But watch out.

Jesus used strong language when confronting these men. He warned: *Woe to you!* The word *woe* means "God's judgment, grief, and denunciation." Why would Jesus do this? After all, the Pharisees walked the dusty streets quoting Scriptures and praying elaborate prayers.

Jesus said that they didn't really love God or others as much as they loved themselves. Actually, they didn't care about other people at all. He pointed to their filthy hearts as their motivation to draw attention to themselves and fool people into believing they were the finest examples of godly men. But they were hypocrites who ordered others around and demanded obedience, yet did not abide by their own rules (Matthew 23).

The Scribes' and Pharisees' appearance of godly behavior led onlookers to believe they had pure hearts. (*Pure* in the Greek means clean, innocent, or guiltless, either literally or ceremonially.) But the Scribes and Pharisees faked their purity. Maybe they didn't recognize their own insincerity. But Jesus did, and He exposed their wicked intentions and motives.

Do we, like a Scribe or Pharisee, sometimes hide a sinful motive? It's difficult and discouraging to face our selfish motives. But we need to do it anyway. We can pray Psalm 51:10: *Create in me a clean heart.*

And 1 John 1:9 assures us *if we confess our sins, He is faithful and righteous to forgive us our sins and to cleanse us from all unrighteousness.* Then we're able to draw near to God with a sincere heart, sprinkled clean and washed with pure water (Hebrews 10:22).

Make It Personal

How would you evaluate yor motives in your curent circumstances? How would God evaluate them?

Today I Bring Praise and Thanksgiving For

Teach Me to Trust You

Read Psalm 25

Key Verses: 25:4–5 *Make me know Your ways, O Lord; Teach me Your paths. Lead me in truth and teach me.*

everal years ago, I was invited to a conference. In preparation for my weekend trip, I asked God to use my time away to teach me what direction I should go with regards to impending decisions.

When I arrived at the hotel, I was given a room on the twenty-eighth floor. After settling in, I opened my Bible and prayed. Three hours passed. I was looking for an epiphany but received no answers.

I closed my Bible, then pulled up a comfy chair and peered out the large picture window that framed a breathtaking sunset. From that height, I could see for miles. Then my attention was drawn below to a traffic jam on the interstate. The road was gridlocked, and cars were backed up for miles. Sirens wailed and emergency vehicles sped by. Instead of the anticipated peaceful view, I saw a disaster on the highway. As cars approached the entrance ramp, I wanted to warn them. From my bird's-eye view, I saw both impending dangers and the better route. I wanted to shout warnings such as

- "Slow down, you don't know what's coming!"
- "If you keep going, you'll wind up in stopped traffic, with no way out!"

- "Hold up! There's a wreck ahead, and you're about to wind up in it!"
- "If you knew what I know, you'd go the other way!"

God then whispered to my heart: *You sound like Me. I know what's on your path. I see impending danger. I know roadblocks that have popped up in your life. But I also know about the potential wreck waiting to happen if you continue on this path. You can trust Me completely to help you find the best route.*

No matter how things look from a human perspective, God knows the right path and what lies in our future. We can ask God for wisdom, knowledge, and understanding (Proverbs 2:6).

Even when it seems we're driving in the dark, we can trust that God knows what He's doing. As God orchestrates the circumstances, we'll learn the right way to go.

Make It Personal

What decision are you making this week? Do you trust God to teach you the best way to go? Why or why not? What can you actively do to show you trust Him today?

Today I Bring Praise and Thanksgiving For

A Heartfelt Examination

Read Psalm 26

Key Verses: 26:2–3 *Examine me, O Lord, and try me; test my mind and my heart.*

Giving my college students an exam was an effective way to measure their learning. Sometimes I gave a pencil-and-paper test; other times I gave an oral exam. Often, the exam was a demonstration of an acquired skill, such as their ability to teach a child to read or make literature come alive.

My job was to determine the value of what my students knew. If there was a concern, we addressed it. If it wasn't right, we fixed it. When these issues were addressed, the student was better equipped to be a teacher of influence and impact.

Regardless of the method of testing, the student had to prove what she had within her heart and mind. Otherwise, I couldn't determine whether or not she was properly prepared.

God is different. He sees the heart — our thoughts and motives. We might attempt to demonstrate how good we are with religious works. Perhaps we speak words lifted from the pages of the Bible, but don't do as they say. God knows the sincerity of our hearts. The Lord said to the prophet Samuel, *"God sees not as man sees, for man looks at the outward appearance, but the Lord looks at the heart"* (1 Samuel 16:7).

God knows the real stuff — the truth behind the desires of our hearts or the motivating factors that drive us forward — even when we don't recognize them. Surrendering our hearts to God can be a frightening moment; we may not want to be completely vulnerable and open with Him. But He already knows our true self and loves us anyway. If there's a problem, God will reveal it. If something isn't right, He'll fix it.

And when our hearts are transformed, then we can become people of influence and impact.

Make It Personal

What, if anything, needs to be changed in your heart?

Today I Bring Praise and Thanksgiving For

Waiting

Read Psalm 27

Key Verse: 27:14 *Wait for the Lord; be strong and let your heart take courage; yes, wait for the Lord.*

*I*n our instant society, we like things done fast. We often consider waiting inconvenient because it tests our patience. We wait for:

- The right relationship
- A new job to begin or retirement to come
- Test results
- Babies to be born and prodigal children to return
- Hardship to end

Yet throughout the Old and New Testaments, we're told to wait in expectation for God to act on our behalf. *To wait* as used in the original Hebrew, means to hope, look eagerly for, expect. Waiting is especially difficult during a season of hardship, but it gives us the opportunity to "exercise" our faith muscles. Waiting also helps us develop a more intimate relationship with Jesus Christ. We can do some beneficial things while we wait:

- Cry out to God. Choose to believe He will hear and answer. Then trust Him.
- Anticipate and expect that God will bring a good result.

- Read the Bible. Meditate on God's promises.
- Hold tight to the hope that God's timing is perfect. God is not in a hurry to produce a perfect result.
- Praise God for His work in the past. Tell others about the good things He has done.
- Be peaceful; do not fret.

Lamentations 3:25 tells us, *The Lord is good to those who wait for Him, to the person who seeks Him.* Do you believe He's good? Author and Bible teacher Charles Stanley writes, "You can trust that if He asks you to wait, He has something more wonderful in mind than you could ever provide for yourself."[9] Now, that is good.

While we wait, let's be encouraged with words from Isaiah 40:31: *Those who wait for the Lord will gain new strength; they will mount up with wings like eagles, they will run and not get tired, they will walk and not become weary.*

Make It Personal

What are you waiting for? Something to begin or something to end? What will you do while you wait?

Today I Bring Praise and Thanksgiving For

Hold Me

Read Psalm 28

Key Verse: 28:2 *Hear the voice of my supplications when I cry to You for help, when I lift up my hands toward Your Holy sanctuary.*

At ages three and seven, when my daughters were walking with our family in the woods one day, my husband recorded the girls' movements with his video camera. The seven-year-old scurried down the path with complete confidence. But the three-year-old stopped abruptly, wheeled around to face the camera, and with arms held high to her daddy said, "Hold me!" At first, my husband replied that his hands were full holding the camera. But she insisted, so he handed the camera to me and picked her up.

Perhaps at some time we've all felt like my three-year-old daughter. We can't continue to walk. The path has become too steep. In our weary state, we can either plop down on the ground, or we can lift our heads and hands up to God and ask Him to hold us.

David was often in a state of turmoil and confusion. And to whom did he turn? He directed his cries to God. As David lamented, he lifted his hands in prayer. The uplifting of hands showed his need, his humility, and his confidence. He knew God was his only help and that God would be faithful and hold him up.

Isaiah 63:9 tells us, *In all their affliction He was afflicted, and the angel of His presence saved them; In His love and in His mercy*

He redeemed them, and He lifted them and carried them all the days of old.

God carries us when the path has become steep, dark, or rocky. He holds our hearts in times of sorrow. He holds our hand so we don't go alone.

Deuteronomy 1:31 tells us, *The Lord your God carried you, as a man carries his son, all the way that you went until you came to this place.* Like David and my daughter, let's lift up our hands and ask for help. Reach for Jesus. He's holding onto us.

Make It Personal

What is the hardest part about asking God to hold you? Reflect on a time you cried out to God. What was His response?

Today I Bring Praise and Thanksgiving For

Unleash the Power Within

Read Psalm 29

Key Verse: 29:4 *The voice of the Lord is powerful.*

During the 2014 CMA Country Christmas show on ABC, Tony Award-winning singer and actress, Idina Menzel, was asked what makes the movie *Frozen* different. She replied, "It's about unleashing the power within." To what kind of power do you think she was referring?

The writer of Psalm 29 clearly identifies God as the mightiest and strongest power source of all.

Our culture uses power in many ways. Power operates our machinery, which then enables our homes to function. Someone who is empowered has the authority to manage people, businesses, and corporations. Money in a bank account may enable someone to buy favor from powerful people. Whether power is abused or used for the greater good, earthly power is available only because God allows it.

David mentions the power of God's voice seven times. The voice of God that created the universe is full of power. The powerful voice in this psalm is not the "still, small voice" of 1 Kings 19:12. Here, God's voice is authoritative. God's voice compels the strike of lightning, makes the cedar tree split, the wilderness shake, and the deer to go into labor.

Acts 1:8 tells us, *You will receive power when the Holy Spirit has come upon you.* When we give our life to God, we're empowered with His Holy Spirit. The same God who powerfully spoke the world into existence and keeps it functioning, provides us with supernatural power to live, work, and operate in this world according to biblical principles.

We may not know the singer's source of power, but we do know ours. The next time you witness a powerful thunderstorm, think of the power of God. Then with confidence, tap into your personal power source, power from Almighty God.

Make It Personal

Do you see God as more powerful than any other earthly or heavenly power? Why or why not?

Today I Bring Praise and Thanksgiving For

Devastated and Disappointed

Read Psalm 30

Key Verse: 30:5 *Weeping may last for the night, but a shout of joy comes in the morning.*

People, circumstances, and events can leave us feeling disappointed — an emotion defined as a "feeling of sadness by the nonfulfillment of one's hopes or expectations." Can you relate?

- You didn't get the raise or promotion you thought you deserved.
- Your child made careless choices.
- You wrote your best paper, but your professor disagreed.
- Your prayer wasn't answered the way you had hoped.

Three siblings — Mary, Martha, and Lazarus — were close friends of Jesus. When Lazarus became sick, the sisters sent a message to Jesus telling him about Lazarus's condition. They expected Jesus, the Healer, to come quickly. But He didn't come for two more days, and by that time, Lazarus had died. When Martha finally saw Jesus she said, *"Lord, if you had been here, my brother would not have died"* (John 11:21).

Is that an attitude we detect? Was she really saying, "It's all your fault!"? Maybe Martha was mad. But at the very least, Martha was disappointed because she believed that if Jesus had been there Lazarus wouldn't have died. She couldn't see past her grief or her disappointment to understand that Jesus had a purpose for His delay. Later Jesus said, *"This is for the glory of God"* (John 11:4.) Lazarus' death and resurrection had a purpose: *Then many believed in Him* (John 11:45).

We don't have to become derailed from God's purpose when we experience disappointment. We can:

- begin to operate out of trust. Read Scriptures declaring that God is trustworthy and in control. Ask God to help us believe.
- move closer to God by praying.
- be honest with God. Remember, He already knows what's inside our hearts.
- ask for wisdom and right thinking.
- boldly tell God we need His help.
- expect to be revived! Isaiah 57:15 tells us that God will revive the spirit of the lowly.

Let's not lose heart. Isaiah 49:23 tells us *those who hopefully wait for Me will not be put to shame.*

Make It Personal

Reflect on a past or current disappointment. What did God teach you then or what do you need God to do now? How would you counsel someone struggling with disappointment?

Today I Bring Praise and Thanksgiving For

Abandoned and Betrayed

Read Psalm 31

Key Verses: 31:11–12 *I have become . . . an object of dread to my acquaintances; those who see me in the street flee from me. I am forgotten as a dead man, out of mind; I am like a broken vessel.*

Do you know a woman whose co-workers exclude her? Or you observe her adversaries snickering behind her back? You suspect she might be lonely, and you think you heard her cry in the bathroom when she thought she was alone.

Gossip flies through the office like bees swarming from a hive. Are the stories truth or falsehood? Doesn't matter. She's already been judged. She is ignored and not invited to join the group. She has done something bad, or said something wrong, or hasn't lived up to others' expectations. Or maybe she's done none of those things. She's just fallen victim to vicious lies.

Perhaps you're that woman.

She, or you, wouldn't be the first.

David said his best friends didn't want to be seen with him anymore. No wonder David cried out that his bones hurt, his eyes were weary, and his strength was gone. His pain was made worse because he was alone, rejected, and dismissed. He felt betrayed.

David did the only thing he knew to do — and it's the very best thing. He poured out his heart to God and then settled into his safe place; he took refuge in the Lord. In his time of immense suffering, David made God his best friend.

And we can too. After all, Jesus was betrayed by Judas (Luke 22:1-6), so He knows first hand how we feel.

When we feel the pain of abandonment, betrayal, gossip, or fabrications, let's take our pain to God. He tells us in Hebrews 13:5, *"I will never desert you, nor will I ever forsake you."*

Co-workers, friends, and even family, may abandon you. But Jesus never will.

Make It Personal

Who do you reach out to when you feel abandoned??

Today I Bring Praise and Thanksgiving For

Running to God

Read Psalm 32

Key Verse: 32:1 *How blessed is he whose transgression is forgiven, whose sin is covered.*

*S*atan is relentless in his pursuit to destroy every Christian's right relationship with God. His device is deception. Satan cunningly plants within our thoughts the lie that our sin is so bad that God can't forgive us. Feeling shame and embarrassment, we conclude that it would be better to run from God and hide. Satan used this same lie in the Garden of Eden. After Adam and Eve disobeyed God, Satan told them to hide. Maybe, then, God wouldn't notice they'd disobeyed Him.

For almost a year David believed the same lie. But his unconfessed sin of adultery, murder, and deceit made him a physical and emotional wreck. In Psalm 32:3 he wrote this: *When I kept silent about my sin, my body wasted away through my groaning all day long.*

Then something incredible happened.

In Psalm 32:4 he wrote, *Day and night Your hand was heavy upon me.* God's love spilled out in the form of conviction — God's heavy hand. God beckoned David to come back. And David ran to God. He wrote, *I acknowledged my sin to You . . . and You forgave the guilt of my sin* (verse 5). Instant forgiveness. No probationary period. Immediate restoration.

We must resist the urge to run from God in shame, denial, fear, or guilt, or we, like David, will waste away. Instead, let's run to God and throw our mistakes into His loving arms. Sin separates us from God. He doesn't want that. He longs to restore our joy. He wants a relationship with us.

In Luke 15:11–32 Jesus told the story about a prodigal son who returned home. Notice how the father responded to the son: *So he [the son] got up and came to his father. But while he was still a long way off, his father saw him and felt compassion for him, and ran and embraced him and kissed him* (Luke 15:20).

What a beautiful picture of love! This picture, in fact, is a picture of how God responds to us when we run to Him.

Make It Personal

Have you ever believed the lie that your sin is too bad to be forgiven? What does God wants you to do?

Today I Bring Praise and Thanksgiving For

In God's Hands

Read Psalm 33

Key Verse: 33:21 *Our heart rejoices in Him, because we trust in His holy name.*

I sat down in the hairdresser's chair after a long day — and it was only noon. I anticipated the stroke of the brush against my head would be calming. I needed to relax. My heart was still heavy, despite praying all morning. I couldn't do what I desired to do — manipulate and take control of a bad situation and, hopefully, make things work out the way I thought they should.

Have you ever felt that way?

In this case, distance and timing made my involvement impossible. Everything was out of my control.

My hairdresser opened a drawer. But she didn't pull out a brush. She lifted a card and handed it to me. I opened the envelope. Inside was a beautiful sterling bookmark engraved with the words, "Trust in the Lord."

At the precise moment I needed it, God spoke. He reminded me that everything was under control because the situation was in His hands. My heart truly became joyful.

Are you a "fixer" like me? Do you long to "help people out"? Although a strong leader himself, David knew that his strength, abilities, and any control he thought he had were as "nothing" compared to God's. God is the only One who makes things happen . . . or not happen. Kings aren't saved because of an army; the warrior's strength cannot save himself; and a horse can't bring victory in war unless God allows it (Psalm 33:16–17). Nothing is in our control; everything is in God's hands.

Some may see my beauty shop appointment and the bookmark as a coincidence, but I know God orchestrated it to answer my prayer and remind me to trust that everything was in His hands.

Make It Personal

What part of your life is the most difficult to release into God's hands?

Today I Bring Praise and Thanksgiving For

Radiate Jesus

Read Psalm 34

Key Verse: 34:5 *They looked to Him and were radiant.*

Practically speaking, what does it mean to radiate God? Can it only happen when one is joyful?

It had been a hard morning. I meandered to the community pool where I could gather my thoughts. My Bible was open on my lap, and I was holding a Bible study guide with my right hand. An older woman got out of the pool, grabbed her towel from the chair beside me, and started drying off. With swollen eyes still wet from tears, I looked her straight in the eye. Despite my sorrow, I smiled.

"It looks like you're studying," she said.

"Yes, I am. Are you familiar with this study?" She glanced down at my Bible and accompanying Bible study book and responded, "Oh no . . . I'm an agnostic."

I knew what that meant, but I wanted to hear it from her. "What does that mean?"

She flung her hands in the air. "Don't know … don't care."

I nodded and continued to smile. "Yeah . . . I believe God created me and has a purpose for me. I'm just experiencing some tough stuff right now. I've received bad news, so I'm reading my Bible, searching for hope."

She continued to dry her back but looked deep into my eyes. "You radiate," she said. "You're the kind of Christian Jesus was talking about."

73

She knew how Jesus defined Christians?

Jesus shone through the cracks of my brokenness, reflecting a holy presence. A woman who didn't care about His existence admitted, "I see Jesus in you."

When David wrote our key verse, he wasn't sitting on a high hill overlooking beautiful meadows, with a cup of hot coffee in his hand. Theologians say David penned this psalm when he was fleeing from Saul, his wicked enemy. David escaped with his men (about four hundred) to the wilderness where they found a cave and went into hiding. In his difficult circumstance, David stayed close to God and knew God was with them.

When times are difficult or we're dealt the unexpected, we can call on God to give us courage and peace. Then when we do, our faces will radiate the presence of God.

Make It Personal

Do you feel you radiate Jesus? Why or why not?

Today I Bring Praise and Thanksgiving For

Rescued from the Enemy

Read Psalm 35

Key Verse: 35:1 *Fight against those who fight against me.*

avid wrote this psalm at a low period in his life. He had just fled from Saul the first time. And he had faked insanity in front of Ablimelech — who eventually let him go. David cried out to God for help against his enemies — who quite possibly were coming over the mountain to attack him. He asked God to rescue him from a bleak situation. We probably don't have an army running through the neighborhood prepared to attack us. But we all have enemies.

The definition of enemy is broad: "one that is antagonistic to another; one seeking to injure, overthrow; something harmful or deadly; a military adversary."

The language in the psalm seems harsh. David pleads for help and payback against his enemies. His real desire is that they get what's coming to them — what they deserve. He calls on God to vindicate him, because he knows God is a righteous judge.

While we all have enemies, our ultimate enemy is Satan. In fact, if you consider these synonyms for enemy — *opponent, adversary, foe, rival, competitor, and antagonist* — Satan fits the description perfectly. John 10:10 tells us that the devil *comes only to steal and kill and destroy.*

An enemy yearns to bring destruction, and the devil will use whatever it takes to make that happen:

- addictions
- a corrupt judicial system
- hostile co-workers
- gossips
- deceivers
- hateful people

The good news is the rest of John 10:10, which tells us Jesus came *that we might have life, and have it abundantly*. God sees and hears the evil. He smells the stench of injustice and He is repulsed. Because we are His children, He cares about our well-being and will come to our defense.

Deuteronomy 20:4 tells us, *the Lord your God is the one who goes with you, to fight for you against your enemies, to save you*. In Psalm 35:10 David wrote, *Lord, who is like You, who delivers the afflicted from him who is too strong for him?* David recognized — and we can too — that God saved him from the enemy.

Make It Personal

Who or what do you consider your enemy?

Today I Bring Praise and Thanksgiving For

God's Chick

Read Psalm 36

Key Verse: 36:7 *How precious is Your lovingkindness, O God! And the children of men take refuge in the shadow of Your wings.*

When a bird sits on its eggs in its nest, its entire body envelopes the tiny eggs, providing them complete protection from storms or predators.

Comparatively, in the shadow of God's wings, we are guarded. Psalm 91:4 reiterates *He will cover you with His feathers, and under His wings you will find refuge; His faithfulness will be your shield and rampart* (NIV).

The Bible doesn't say God has wings; rather, *wings* is used as a metaphor to describe God's protection. This Scripture picture shows God's love and how willing and able He is to shield us. Our part is to trust Him. His part is to protect.

Similarly, a mother hen protects her chicks by fluffing her feathers so she appears much larger. When enemies come close, she's a huge fluff ball that flaps her wings and makes a racket so enemies fly away.

Sometimes, though, we may be like the wayward chick that runs loose on the farm. We run away from God's protection. Luke 13:34 tells us Jesus said, *"How often I wanted to gather your children together, just as a hen gathers her brood under her wings, and you would not have it!"*

How often do we run through life seeking protection in other people and things?

When the storms of adversity gather or the predators seek to devour, we can be overcome with fear, or we can acknowledge Psalm 63:7: *You have been my help, and in the shadow of Your wings I sing for joy.*

Let's be God's chick and sing for joy as we nestle under His strong, protective wings.

Make It Personal

In what ways could you say you have "been running loose" away from the safety of God's protection?

Today I Bring Praise and Thanksgiving For

A Tweet from Heaven

Read Psalm 37

Key Verse: 37:7 *Rest in the Lord and wait patiently for Him; do not fret because of him who prospers in his way.*

*S*he captivated me for thirty minutes, early one spring morning. Back and forth, the mama bird flitted and tweeted, bringing succulent grubs to her babies. Her persistent effort to scrounge food for her babies amazed me. God knew my heart was heavy. He knew that mama bird's faithfulness would bring His Word back to me.

Matthew 6:26–27 tells us, *Look at the birds of the air, that they do not sow, nor reap nor gather into barns, and yet your heavenly Father feeds them. Are you not worth much more than they? And who of you by being worried can add a single hour to his life?*

Fretting is defined as "worrying" or "an agitation of mind." Bible dictionaries convey that *fret* means "consume." Fretting is being consumed with worry.

Why do we worry? Do we wear worry like a badge of honor because we think it means we care more?

According to the National Institute of Health (NIH) stress causes health problems including: weak immune system, high blood pressure, ulcers and acid reflux, increase in blood sugar levels, migraines, respiratory problems, and so much more.[10] Jesus wants to keep us from these worry-related health issues. First Peter 5:7 tells us, *Cast all your anxiety on [Jesus], because He cares for you.*

He cares about every part of us, including our physical and emotional health.

The baby birds didn't think about where their nourishment would come from. They trusted their mama. Will we trust our heavenly Father as much? As we feed on His Word, He breathes life into our starved emotional and physical state.

Take pen to paper and make a list of anything that is causing you to fret. Then read your list to God and say, "God, you tell me in Matthew 6:25 not to worry. So, I'm giving You my worries. Thank you for taking care of me just like you care for the birds."

Make It Personal

What causes you to fret? What is God tweeting you today?

Today I Bring Praise and Thanksgiving For

The Sin of Selfishness

Read Psalm 38

Key Verses: 38:4, 18 *My iniquities are gone over my head; as a heavy burden they weigh too much for me . . . . I confess my iniquity; I am full of anxiety because of my sin.*

*D*avid was miserable. He had festering wounds, fever, inflammation, and searing pain. His vision was blurred and his hearing was failing. His emotional state was as bad — anguish wracked his heart. In this case, David's sickness and suffering were a result of his sinful choices. He denied his sinful actions for one year, burying the reality of his sin in his heart. Why?

David might have believed that by ignoring his sin it was as if it never happened. Or maybe he didn't think confession was important. Look no further to find the definition of selfishness — David put himself and his desires before God during this season of life (2 Samuel 11:1–27).

Is confession necessary? Didn't Christ's death and resurrection take the penalty for our sin already?

Author and Bible teacher John MacArthur explains that judicial forgiveness was purchased by Christ's death on the cross. But God also extends another kind of forgiveness.[11]

God takes displeasure when His children sin. Confession is necessary because sin has a penalty. Hebrews 12:6 tells us, *The Lord disciplines the one He loves, and chastises every son whom He receives* (ESV).

81

Selfishness always leads to sin. Adultery, deception to gain success, jealousy or dissatisfaction that prompts compromising our morals, selfishness lies at the root of all.

David wrapped up his honest rant with confession. He accepted God's forgiveness and restoration began. David overcame. So can we.

Psalm 103:12 tells us, *As far as the east is from the west, so far has He [God] removed our transgressions from us.*

Like David, we can acknowledge our sin and trust God to remove it from us. Healing and restoration will always follow.

Make It Personal

Are you in denial about any sin? If yes, ask God to help you identify it.

Today I Bring Praise and Thanksgiving For

Our Tongue: A Weapon or a Tool

Read Psalm 39

Key Verse: 39:1 *I will guard my ways that I may not sin with my tongue; I will guard my mouth as with a muzzle.*

The adage "sticks and stones may break my bones but words can never hurt me," originated in 1892.[12] The saying was meant to help those being bullied by insults. Today we better understand the harmful effects of cruel words. Proverbs 12:18 tell us that words used in a wrong or hurtful way pierce like a sword.

Hurtful words are spoken in nearly every private or social setting. They can be abrupt and intentional, or they may creep into the conversation in a subtle, unplanned way. Christians are not excluded. In the name of a prayer request, we might share details that shouldn't be shared. We may unknowingly discuss situations with people who listen only for the purpose of obtaining information.

We've watched children endure through the pain of hurtful criticism and verbal insults. We've personally experienced the heartache of insensitive, careless words. And if we're honest, most of us have participated in gossip and criticism, too.

When we examine our inconsiderate words, we discover this truth: Words can ignite a fire that leaves lifetime scars.

David understood the powerful effects of the tongue. That's why he opened this psalm declaring that in order to avoid sin, he needed to muzzle his mouth.

James 3:5–6 compares our tongue to a spark that escalates into a raging fire, capable of killing a relationship, ruining a reputation, and destroying a Christian's witness. The tongue controls the direction our life takes and is capable of triggering a symbolic emotional death.

We can choose to use our tongue as a weapon to bring destruction or as a tool that speaks words to enrich a person's life. With God's help, our words can be pleasing in His sight (Psalm 19:14). Let's make that our prayer today.

Make It Personal

When have you been affected by someone else's words — spoken, typed, or texted? When do you find it most difficult to muzzle your mouth? What do you think would happen if everyone prayed Psalm 39:1 every day?

Today I Bring Praise and Thanksgiving For

Purpose in Pain

Read Psalm 40

Key Verse: 40:17 *Since I am afflicted and needy, let the Lord be mindful of me. You are my help and my deliverer; do not delay, O my God.*

Rarely are we naturally joyful when pain interrupts our lives. Suffering can be an intruder who comes unexpectedly and slams us against a wall. Or pain can creep in and push us downward into a miry pit.

However, suffering can be a time of gaining valuable insights. Second Corinthians 4:16–17 tells us, *Therefore we do not lose heart, but though our outer man is decaying, yet our inner man is being renewed day by day. For momentary, light affliction is producing for us an eternal weight of glory far beyond all comparison.*

When suffering comes:

- Identify the source. If your pain was caused by another person's choices, trust that your current suffering has been allowed by God. Resist the urge to complain. Instead, ask God to reveal what He wants you to learn.

- Determine if suffering was brought on by your wrong choices. If so, ask for God's forgiveness. Be ready for a new start. Hebrews 12:11 tells us, *All discipline for the moment seems not to be joyful, but sorrowful; yet to those who have been trained by it, afterwards it yields the peaceful fruit of righteousness.* Even when you experience the consequences of sin, God will sustain you.

85

- Believe God works all things together for good. This doesn't imply all things *are* good in themselves, but collectively, all things *become* good in the sense that God will use them to produce the right outcome (Romans 8:28).

- Pray daily. The next morning when it still hurts, pray again.

- Trust God's mysterious ways. From a human vantage point, it's impossible to perceive all God is doing or what He may have prevented.

In pain, we have opportunity to realize God's attributes — His faithfulness, strength, compassion, and mercy — first-hand. To know God is faithful is good. To experience His faithfulness is great.

Make It Personal

How will you use these promises in your suffering?

Today I Bring Praise and Thanksgiving For

Heal My Soul

Read Psalm 41

Key Verse: 41:4 *O Lord, be gracious to me; heal my soul, for I have sinned against you.*

*S*itting in the sauna was exactly what my body needed. I'd read about the benefits:

- Rising body temperature promotes heart health, resembling mild exercise.
- Deep sweating releases toxins in the body.
- Perspiration cleans bacteria from our skin.
- Higher body temperatures produce white blood cells that help fight cold, flu, sinus congestion, and allergies.[13]

I needed to be refreshed and cleansed. My sweat-drenched skin glistened. Perspiration beaded on my forehead and dripped from my face. Sprinkled with water this way, I felt clean.

To be fully refreshed, we also need a spiritual cleansing. Sin is toxic in our bodies, and unresolved guilt weighs heavy on our hearts. Both activate breakdowns that affect all areas of our lives. Like the release of toxins through sweat, we can release the sin that makes our heart, soul, and mind sick.

We become truly clean when we pray, *wash me thoroughly from my iniquity and cleanse me from my sin* (Psalm 51:2). In the Hebrew, the words *healing* and *cleansed* both mean "to be purified." We can be purified, totally clean — "washed whiter than snow" (Psalm 51:7).

Ezekiel 36:25 tells us, *Then I will sprinkle clean water on you, and you will be clean; I will cleanse you from all your filthiness and from all your idols.*

Admitting that we've sinned might not be easy, but it's a necessary step to confession. When we ask the Lord to be gracious or merciful, we're asking Him to withhold the punishment we deserve for the sin we've committed. Confession leads to the healing of our souls.

Like the cleansing beads of sweat, words of confession wash away all the filthiness. We won't glisten with sweat, but we'll radiate with joy because of a healed heart.

Make It Personal

Is your heart heavy? Is a sinful attitude, habit, disposition, or action making you feel dirty? If so, what is the root cause?

Today I Bring Praise and Thanksgiving For

Sustaining Hope

Read Psalm 42

Key Verse: 42:11 *Why are you in despair, O my soul? And why have you become disturbed within me? Hope in God, for I shall yet praise Him, the help of my countenance and my God.*

Do you sometimes feel hopeless?

A 2012 *Psychology Today* article reported that about six percent of the population feels a sense of hopelessness.[14] In our humanity, we tell ourselves:

- I'm weary. But God's Word says, *I satisfy the weary ones and refresh everyone who languishes* (Jeremiah 31:25).

- I can't do it. But God's Word says, *[You] can do all things through Him* (Philippians 4:13).

- I'll never make it. But God's Word says, *[You're] being strengthened with all power according to his glorious might so that you may have great endurance and patience* (Colossians 1:11).

- I'm doomed. But God's Word says, *[You're] struck down, but not destroyed* (2 Corinthians 4:9.)

- It'll never work out. But God's Word says, *Is anything too difficult for the Lord?* (Genesis 18:14).

- I'm weak. But God's Word says, *My grace is sufficient for you, for my power is made perfect in weakness. Therefore I will boast all the more gladly of my weaknesses, so that the power of Christ may rest on me (2 Corinthians 12:9).*

The Dictionary of Bible Theology gives many meanings for the word *hope*: to trust, have patience, and wait with expectation.[15]

This hope — God's hope — is the hope we need at all times, especially when we're in despair. This hope gives us reason to get up in the morning. The promises of God enable us to tell ourselves new truths:

Life will get better.

My situation is going to turn around.

God is always with me and He can do everything.

I can't see any benefit, but God sees the whole picture.

God is helping me see the light in the darkness.

Most likely, statements like these won't immediately change the situation. But this cheerleader type-talk (as I like to call it) changes our attitude and provides hope. Without this hope, we'd sink.

When we're in despair, God — perfect and powerful — is the hope we need to sustain us.

Make It Personal

Back to the initial question: Are you feeling hopeless? Which of these Scriptures brought you encouragement today?

Today I Bring Praise and Thanksgiving For

A Terrible, Horrible, No Good, Very Bad Day

Read Psalm 43

Key Verse: 43:5 *Why are you in despair, O my soul? And why are you disturbed within me? Hope in God, for I shall again praise Him, the help of my countenance and my God.*

*I*f there's ever been a children's book that King David could have written it would be, *Alexander and the Terrible, Horrible, No Good, Very Bad Day* by Judith Viorst. David had more than one horrible day.

I read this book to my children many times. I wanted to teach them that we all have bad days. But, I think I'm the one who learned the most from Alexander. His bad day included:

- experiencing the repercussions of poor choices.
- being bombarded with unforeseen problems at the break of dawn.
- disappointment . . . again and again.
- everyone else's work was better.
- being slighted by a best friend and then abandoned.
- an unexpected medical condition.

- being picked on by peers.
- no one would listen.

Alexander, David, and us. We all know how to define a horrible day, or a bad season in life. Unlike Alexander, though, David had a tried and proven antidote to ease his suffering: He put on the attitude of praise.

British Prime Minister Winston Churchill once said, "Attitude is a little thing that makes a big difference." From a downcast perspective, we see only our problems, and they appear to be huge. Feeling overwhelmed with despair keeps us from living a victorious life.

In the children's story, Alexander was made to put on pajamas he didn't like. Isaiah 61:3 tells us to put on *praise instead of a spirit of fainting* so we have the proper attitude. Psalm 100:4 tells us to *enter His gates with thanksgiving and His courts with praise.* We may feel like fainting from the weariness this life brings, but an attitude of praise transports us into the presence of God where our strength is renewed.

Make It Personal

Is this a bad day? Season? Why or why not? In what ways can you praise God?

Today I Bring Praise and Thanksgiving For

Connect the Dots

Read Psalm 44

Key Verse: 44:1 *O God, we have heard with our ears, our fathers have told us the work that You did in their days, in the days of old.*

When I was in the fourth grade and living in California, two life-changing events occurred. First, I trusted Jesus as my Savior. Second, my family took a six-week vacation and traveled to every state in the United States.

My life fell apart two years later when my parents divorced and Mom moved us to North Carolina — the state she fell in love with on our family vacation. During the autumn of my sixth-grade year, God brought a friend into my life, who invited me to her church. The following year the pastor invited me to take a sign language class. I loved signing and spent the next five years interpreting for the deaf at church.

My senior year of high school arrived. Due to the lack of finances, a college education seemed unobtainable, especially at the Christian college I longed to attend. Heartbroken, I felt hopeless — until I received that call from someone at that college. They needed interpreters for their deaf students, and the compensation I would receive nearly equaled a full-ride scholarship.

God tells us in Isaiah 65:24, *"I will answer them before they call to me. While they are still talking about their prayers, I will go ahead and answer their prayers"* (NLT).

God still works in this way today. Hindsight really is 20/20.

When we connect the dots between our past and present, we see how God made connections to fulfill His purpose for us.

The psalmist tells us to remember God's amazing work in our lives and to tell others what He did. God will receive glory, and listeners will be encouraged. And when we feel worried or uncertain, we can recall how God took care of us in the past and trust that He'll take care of us in our present situation.

Let's connect our personal dots today. By doing so, God will be glorified, and we'll have hope for the future.

Make It Personal

Connect your dots. What event do you recall that was nothing short of a miracle? When has God intervened and answered a prayer? Who can you tell about the wonderful things God has done in your past?

Today I Bring Praise and Thanksgiving For

The Fragrance of New Life

Read Psalm 45

Key Verses: 45:7–8 *Therefore God, Your God, has anointed You with the oil of joy above Your fellows. All Your garments are fragrant with myrrh and aloes and cassia.*

The sense of smell enriches our lives. With it we experience the pleasure of tasty food. The smell of lavender might envelope us with peace. Citrus might flood our hearts with joy. Some smells create a memory. One person recalled, "Honeysuckle transports me back to my youth when school was out and summer was just beginning."

Some people, like me, lather their bodies with fragranced lotions. We massage essential oils onto our body to soften our skin. They may provide a calming sensation and emit a lovely aroma too.

On the other hand synthetic fragrances, included in many perfumes and colognes, lotions, and many other products, can be toxic and make people physically ill or lead to death.

Natural fragrances have been used since the beginning of time, as seen in this wedding psalm. During biblical times, the Jewish bridegroom went to his bride's home to claim her on their wedding day. The psalmist says, the bride is clothed in not only gold, but also with fragranced oils and perfumes.

If we're a Christ-follower, we're described as the "bride of Christ" (John 3:29). One day Jesus will return and claim His bride. What will our fragrance be like?

Second Corinthians 2:14–15 tells us, *But thanks be to God, who always leads us in triumph in Christ, and manifests through us the sweet aroma of the knowledge of Him in every place . . . For we are a fragrance of Christ.*

The Gospel message is like incense diffused everywhere. Those who live for Christ share the Gospel and emit His love. This lovely fragrance rises up to God. Those who reject Christ reject the fragrance and the result is death. But those who receive the gospel become the fragrance of new life in Christ.

The more we become like Christ, the more we become the fragrance of this new life. Can others smell the fragrance of Christ in us? Today, let's ask God to help us be a sweet-smelling aroma to others.

Make It Personal

What needs to die in your life so that you'll emit a life-giving aroma to those around you? When people get a whiff of you, is the scent you exude nauseating or uplifting?

Today I Bring Praise and Thanksgiving For

The Squirrel's Life

Read Psalm 46

Key Verse: 46:10 *Cease striving and know that I am God.*

I watched as they scrambled in the wooded part of my yard. Dozens of squirrels moving around like they couldn't make up their mind about what to do, how fast to move, or where to go. They dug in the ground, scurried up trees, and chased each other. Except for one.

That squirrel sat motionless on a short limb protruding from the side of a tall oak tree. I wondered if he deliberately put himself there. I watched a few seconds longer, then concluded that in his "stillness" he was resting, refusing to participate in the confusion.

Some days, the scurrying squirrels resemble my life.

Particular seasons require us to be busier than others. It could be a temporary situation, or it might be a deliberate, chosen habit. Regardless, we each must get a sense of what busyness looks like in our lives, how it affects us and the people we love, and how we can best deal with it. When we become too busy, though, it's easier to overlook the joy of the task because of our busy state of mind. Even when our bodies momentarily stop — maybe at a red light — our minds continue to move in fast-forward, looking ahead to the next task. Not much joy in that.

Our key verse instructs us to *cease striving*. In the NIV it's *be still*.

Like the squirrel on his private limb, we need to pull away to our private place and ask God to help us find that balance between work and relaxation, and help us refocus. In *Matthew 11:28 Jesus says, "Come to Me, all who are weary and heavy-laden, and I will give you rest."*

We can choose to scramble with the dozens of squirrels in our circle. Or we can be like the squirrel who goes out on a private limb to find rest and solitude.

Make It Personal

Are you a scrambling squirrel or a still one?

Today I Bring Praise and Thanksgiving For

Yay, God!

Read Psalm 47

Key Verse: 47:1 *O clap your hands, all peoples; shout to God with the voice of joy.*

Can you hear the applause? It roars throughout the sports arena when fans cheer for their team. Whether we're watching a Broadway show or a hometown movie, clapping breaks the silence when we're emotionally moved. Hand-clapping and verbal shouts of praise accompany the crowning of a beauty queen.

Even observing a baby's first steps compels us to break out into sudden claps of joy. We applaud when we're supporting our children's sporting events or dance recitals, when they make good grades or catch their first fish. Honoring others for their high achievement and success brings us to our feet with praise.

Do we admire God's work as much? Have you ever clapped for God? He is the only One truly worthy of recognition. Have you ever watched a glorious sunrise spread its color across the sky and broke out into spontaneous applause? When God performs a miracle in your life, do you ever clap and shout, "Yay, God"?

Be reminded:

- God rained down bread from heaven. (Exodus 16:4)

- He created the stars. (Isaiah 40:26)

- All things came into being through Him. (John 1:3)

- He made the heavens and earth . . . nothing is too hard for God. (Jeremiah 32:17)

No one is more deserving of a loud, enthusiastic standing ovation, than our God. Oh, how He must enjoy the sounds of praises when we clap loudly and tell Him how worthy He is!

Eventually, every person and every nation will shout accolades to God as they bow at His throne (Philippians 2:10). What a privilege and honor it is to praise Him now.

All we need to do is stand to our feet, look to heaven, and break out in applause.

Make It Personal

What will you applaud God for today?

Today I Bring Praise and Thanksgiving For

The Victorious City

Read Psalm 48

Key Verse: 48:2 *Beautiful in elevation, the joy of the whole earth, is Mount Zion in the far north. The city of the great King.*

Waiting in the checkout line at the grocery store I overheard an older man and woman discussing recent events. They didn't appear to know each other, but both were drawn to the news headlines. Having read a headline about reckless decisions affecting our city, the man confidently replied, "God is in control." With a puzzled look, the woman replied, "I don't think so."

The people in Psalm 48 were talking about their own city — but they had a different outlook from the woman who denied God was in control. These people loved God and trusted Him to protect their city. They stood tall with pride as they celebrated the victory Jehovah God brought them. The people were filled with gratitude and they responded to God's faithfulness with worship and praise. They acknowledged their victory was not because the city was built with strong bricks, but rather because it had been built by a strong God.

Today, people continue to build cities. Some have turned away from biblical principles and made other things more important than God. This may provoke a response of fear. From our limited perspective, it may appear people are rejecting Christian values. We may feel we are drowning in a hate-driven, depraved society.

Wiersbe says, "The greatest danger a nation faces is not the invading enemy on the outside but the eroding enemy on the inside — a people gradually turning away from the faith of their fathers."[16]

Regardless of our current surroundings, God still desires to lead. Why? Because He loves us. Today, we have peace and joy not because of what we see around us, but because of what we don't see — a sovereign God who is totally in control.

The Lord declares in Zachariah 2:5, *"I will be a wall of fire around her, and I will be the glory in her midst."*

Make It Personal

In what ways do you see God's control in your city? How do you find joy when faced with uncertainty and fear? How will you pray for your city?

Today I Bring Praise and Thanksgiving For

Different but the Same

Read Psalm 49

Key Verse: 49:17 *When he dies he will carry nothing away; his glory will not descend after him.*

All kinds and classes of people make up our world:

- that dejected woman in India
- that man at his desk in the topmost office on Wall Street
- that Hollywood star walking inconspicuously, her face hidden behind her sunglasses
- the old lady down the street sweeping her porch
- the doctor saving a child's life
- the musician holding the golden trophy
- the athlete wearing the ribbon
- the teacher in Mexico
- the factory worker walking to work
- the executive being picked up in a limo

People are diverse with stark difference in lifestyles. But we are completely identical too — we all will eventually die. Power cannot prevent death. Social class, money, possessions — nothing we have can stop death. Potions and magic won't block the inevitable.

Yet, the world is obsessed with getting wealth, achieving

success, and becoming powerful. It's not a sin to have money; it's a sin when money "has us." It's a sin when we take God off the throne of our lives and replace Him with a selfish desire to be rich and powerful.

When we see others with bigger houses, fancy cars, luxurious vacations, and the appearance of fame and power, we shouldn't judge or be jealous. We don't know the condition of their hearts, how they acquired their assets, or how they are using them. That is between them and God.

Having wealth or a powerful position isn't what's at stake. Wiersbe reminds us, "Whatever we have — earn it honestly, spend it wisely, and invest it faithfully in that which pleases the Lord."[17]

Still, whether we have a little or a lot, we leave every acquired thing behind, including our legacy. We take only what endures eternally — our work for Christ (1 Corinthians 3:11-15).

Make It Personal

How are you investing in your spiritual future?

Today I Bring Praise and Thanksgiving For

More Than Empty Words

Read Psalm 50

Key Verse: 50:15 *Call upon Me in the day of trouble; I shall rescue you, and you will honor Me.*

I dropped a penny down the garbage disposal and turned it on before I realized what I'd done. After turning the disposal off, my husband and I both tried to retrieve it by reaching down into the disposal but the chewed-up penny was stuck. The next day, I tried again, but to no avail. When my husband came home from work, however, he had a new idea. Using a flashlight, he spotted the penny stuck inside a crevice. He then chewed a piece of gum, stuck it to the point of a wooden utensil, and pushed it into the garbage disposal. The penny came right up out of the disposal.

"You're so clever to fix it like that," I said.

"It's just good we had a piece of gum," he replied.

"What good is gum if you don't know how to use it?" I quipped.

A pack of gum on the counter might not seem like the obvious tool for clearing an obstruction, but a problem-solver applied his wisdom and recognized another way it could be used.

Likewise, God gives us His wisdom in the Bible. But what good are words if we don't use them, apply them, or obey them and call on God? Knowledge alone isn't enough. Even Satan and his demons know what's written in the Word. Atheists can be equally knowledgeable. They can know who begot whom, every date, and the order of events. But because they lack the Holy Spirit's guidance and teaching, they have facts without wisdom; they have knowledge, but lack understanding. They have empty words . . . words without meaning.

God's Word carries meaning, and He intends for it to change our lives. In His Word we possess what we need to live a righteous life. God wants to show us the way and to help us in every task; being independent and self-reliant is not His way. We must never feel guilty about calling on God every day because that is what He wants us to do.

The stick of gum was a creative way of fixing a single problem. But understanding and applying God's Word — and obediently calling upon God — will transform one's life for eternity.

Make It Personal

Reflect: How has applying God's Word made a difference in your life recently?

Today I Bring Praise and Thanksgiving For

Because We Love Him

Read Psalm 51

Key Verses: 51:16–17 *You do not delight in sacrifice, otherwise I would give it; You are not pleased with burnt offering. The sacrifices of God are a broken spirit; A broken and a contrite heart, O God, You will not despise.*

Walking with me into my bedroom, Lanie, my four-year-old granddaughter spotted my jewelry box.

"Nana," she asked. "Can I look at your jewelry?"

I put the jewelry box on the floor so she could have a closer look.

Clutching dangling silver earrings, she asked, "Where did you get these?"

"From a friend," I said.

"Why?"

"Because she loves me."

Clinching a dazzling gold heart with a red stone, she asked, "Where did you get this?"

"From your mommy."

"Why?"

"Because she loves me."

Picking up a gold ring she asked, "Where did you get this?"

"My mom gave it to me. It was her high school ring."

"Why?"

"Because she loves me."

Holding a diamond heart, she asked, "Where did you get this?"

"From your papa."

"Why?"

"Because he loves me."

With a sweet but curious countenance, she asked, "Does everybody love you?"

I laughed. "Yes, I suppose they do."

Thoughtfully, she put the jewelry back in the box.

With wide eyes, she peered into my eyes and said, "I will bring you something too."

Lanie's heart told her that because she loves me she wanted to bring me something.

What can we give God to show we love Him? When we love God, and put Him first in our lives, we will offer Him a contrite heart — a heart that expresses remorse for sin with a true desire for change. The heart we give Him will be:

- A heart that is humbly dependent on Him
- A heart that trusts Him fully
- A heart that longs to obey
- A heart that is thankful

And our prayer will be verse 10: *Create in me a clean heart, O God, and renew a steadfast spirit within me.*

Make It Personal

Have you given your heart to God? Is there anything in your life you need to release?

Today I Bring Praise and Thanksgiving For

Like an Olive Tree

Read Psalm 52

Key Verse: 52:8 *As for me, I am like a green olive tree in the house of God.*

Many of us consume olives — green, yellow, or black. But did you know the olive has existed and been cultivated by humans for over 5,000 years? Olive trees can live for centuries and remain productive as long as they are pruned correctly. If a tree dies back due to extreme cold, or fire, its roots survive. It regenerates itself and produces new trees. Some of the olive trees in the Garden of Gethsemane date back to the time of Jesus!

Our key verse tells us we're like an olive tree:

- Regardless of the tree's environment — hot, dry, cold, wet, rocky, sandy — the olive tree survives and thrives. Because the roots never die, the olive tree symbolizes perseverance and steadfastness. When pruned, they remain productive. Despite our surroundings, we too, survive and thrive and remain steady.

- An olive tree's blooms produce a fragrance. We're the fragrance of Christ (2 Corinthians 2:15) and produce the beautiful fruit of love, peace, joy, patience, kindness, goodness, faithfulness, gentleness and self-control (Galatians 5:22).

- The oil and leaves from the olive branch bring healing. Similarly, our inspiring, encouraging words can promote healing in a weary soul.
- Olive fruit tastes good and enhances dishes. As believers we have the potential to flavor and enhance another person's life.
- Durable and colorful, olive wood also has interesting grain patterns. Bowls, cutting boards, and other useful items are valued by those who made and use them. We, too, are valued by God who makes us each with a unique purpose (Psalm 139:13-14 and Jeremiah 1:4-5).
- Olive oil is used as fuel in lamps. Matthew 5:14 tells us, *You are the light of the world. A city set on a hill cannot be hidden.*

To sum up, the olive tree symbolizes life — and we do too.

Make It Personal

In what ways is your life symbolic of an olive tree?

Today I Bring Praise and Thanksgiving For

Fear That Stifles

Read Psalm 53

Key Verse: 53:5 *There they were in great fear where no fear had been.*

*D*id you know Thomas Edison was afraid of the dark? His fear propelled him to discover a way we could live in the light. His fear didn't suppress him — he pushed through it and his discovery of the light bulb changed the world.

Satan uses fear to destroy the confidence God gives us to pursue our dreams, passions, and purpose. When fear arises, God wants us to come to Him. He wants to rid us of our fear and replace it with courage. This boldness allows us to push forward and conquer something unknown or pull back and discontinue something that's been a hindrance.

We might fear:

- beginning a new ministry.
- our children moving away from home.
- stepping away from security in something other than God.
- starting a new career or ending one.

Sometimes opportunities come up suddenly or unexpectedly, much like a storm. The transition between our current situation — which may feel calm — and a new opportunity may feel risky or uncomfortable. The fear that accompanies these emotions can stifle us, preventing us from moving forward in God's will.

Procrastination and intimidation will not propel us into God's plan. Neither will dreaming, wishing, or hoping. Fear prevents us from succeeding in God's plans. We need to take action — in the right order. The first step is to look to God for guidance and peace. He tells us in Joshua 1:5, *Just as I have been with Moses, I will be with you; I will not fail you or forsake you.* We can depend on God to faithfully provide wisdom and strength as we execute His plans.

Fear will steal our purpose and passion and leave us in the dark. Hold tight to God's truth found in Isaiah 41:10: *Do not fear, for I am with you; do not anxiously look about you, for I am your God. I will strengthen you, surely I will help you, surely I will uphold you with My righteous right hand.*

Let's allow God to illuminate our darkness.

Make It Personal

How will you apply God's truth in a fearful situation?

Today I Bring Praise and Thanksgiving For

Lord, Help Me

Read Psalm 54

Key Verse: 54:4 *Surely God is my help; the Lord is the one who sustains me.*

How would you fill in this blank? Lord, help me with _____.

Sometimes adults forget the simplest, yet most profound, truths. While I was teaching a fifth-grade class, God used Austin to remind me that God would always help me. I was waiting for an important text — one that concerned an issue I'd been praying about for a year. My phone was visible, and I glanced at it when it vibrated. When I read the simple phrase of good news, tears welled up in my eyes. Thinking the incident had gone unnoticed I proceeded with my work. Austin, a handsome boy with dark hair and tons of freckles, got up from his seat and walked to me. Our eyes locked and he said, "Jesus will always help you."

Simple. Subtle. Truth.

Nehemiah was a man who needed help, too. His heart was burdened for his people, and he knew God had called him to accomplish a huge task amid great difficulties. What did Nehemiah do?

- He prayed to God.
- He confessed sin.

- He fasted and remained steadfast and focused.
- He praised God.

And God's will came to pass. (See Nehemiah 1:1–2:8.)

We must be equally as persistent in our pursuit for help. We weren't meant to be self-sufficient. We were made to need God's help in all things, big and small. No other person or god can do what Almighty God can do. In fact, in Psalm 60:11 David prays, *Give us help from trouble, for the help of man is useless.* Both Nehemiah and David called out to a powerful God for help, then remained confident God would see them through their troubles. And that's what God did.

Are we as confident? Today, let's be as smart as a fifth-grader and trust that Jesus will always help us.

Make It Personal

Go back to our opening question: What do you need God to help you with today?

Today I Bring Praise and Thanksgiving For

Peace That Only Jesus Can Give

Read Psalm 55

Key Verse: 55:18 *He will redeem my soul in peace from the battle which is against me.*

Much of the chaos that takes place in our communities is out of our control. When wickedness runs rampant, our schools, communities, finances, and mental health can be affected. We don't ask for the chaos that's created, but when evil takes place, it can hit close to home.

The *Oxford English Dictionary* defines *chaos* as "complete disorder and confusion."[18] Synonyms include pandemonium, turmoil, mess, and madness. Can you relate to a day of chaos?

On the other hand, *peace* is defined as "freedom from disturbance; tranquility." Synonyms include calm, quiet, stillness, and serenity. Have you had a day of peace? Do you need one?

While we live in a sinful, chaotic world, we can still experience peace. Philippians 4:6–7 tells us, *Be anxious for nothing, but in everything by prayer and supplication with thanksgiving let your requests be made known to God. And the peace of God, which surpasses all comprehension, will guard your hearts and your minds in Christ Jesus.*

Can you conceptualize peace that *surpasses all comprehension*? I can't explain peace without sharing about a horrifying

115

personal experience. The pain was the deepest I'd ever felt. It cut me like a knife. My father had been robbed and murdered. Shock numbed my body. My screams echoed through the house. I wailed.

But wait . . . this isn't about my temporary sorrow, so don't feel sorry for me. This is a story for God's glory.

On that horrible day, I was within weeks of giving birth. Worried about stress levels for both myself and my baby, I cried out to God and asked for peace. There aren't words to describe the peace that enveloped me throughout the weeks that followed — a peace that stayed with me through the birth of my healthy child.

In John 14:27 we read: *Peace I leave with you; My peace I give to you; not as the world gives do I give to you. Do not let your heart be troubled, nor let it be fearful.*

I was the recipient of unpredictable chaos produced by a wicked person. No counselor, therapist, or teacher in this world can provide the peace only Jesus can give.

Make It Personal

In what area do you need peace?

Today I Bring Praise and Thanksgiving For

Tears in a Bottle

Read Psalm 56

Key Verse: 56:8 *You have taken account of my wanderings; put my tears in Your bottle.*

What makes you cry? Do you cry when you're happy or when you're sad? Are you crying now? Have you ever been crying on the inside but unable to shed a tear?

Tears flow easily for some. They cry when they're delighted and they weep when they're sad. We may shed tears when people surprise us with kindness or overwhelm us with love. Sometimes we cry when the helpless hurt.

Archaeologists have discovered small "tear bottles" which mourners used to collect their tears, then bury them at a gravesite. With this bottle was a note that explained their deep sorrow.

Tears in a bottle is a remembrance. God's Word tells us that He chronicles our tears. To think that God not only sees our sorrows but also remembers them could move us to tears. The Lord says in Exodus 3:7, *"I have surely seen the affliction of My people . . . for I am aware of their sufferings."*

God is a compassionate Father who weeps with us. When Jesus felt sorrow and compassion at the death of Lazarus, He wept. John 11:33–35 tells us, *When Jesus therefore saw her weeping, and the Jews who came with her also weeping, He was deeply moved in spirit and was troubled, and said, "Where have you laid him?" They said to Him, "Lord, come and see." Jesus wept.*

While on earth Jesus shed tears. Hebrews 5:7 tells us, *In the days of His flesh, He offered up both prayers and supplications with loud crying and tears to the One able to save Him from death, and He was heard because of His piety.*

God hears our cries. And our tears mean something to Him. If they didn't, He wouldn't keep count of them.

And remember, Revelation 21:4 tells us *He will wipe every tear from their eyes.* Hold these truths tightly today.

Make It Personal

What makes you weep — on the outside or the inside?

Today I Bring Praise and Thanksgiving For

His Shadow

Read Psalm 57

Key Verse: 57:1 *Be gracious to me, O God, be gracious to me, for my soul takes refuge in You; and in the shadow of Your wings I will take refuge until destruction passes by.*

"Lanie is always in my shadow," my daughter says. "Right with me at all times." Mother and daughter — always together, close in heart and near in proximity.

In our key verse, David's desire was to be kept in God's shadow. To fully grasp the significance, read how both *Dictionary.com* and the *Bible Dictionary* define *shadow*:

- a "dark figure or image cast on the ground or some surface by a body intercepting light; overspread with shadow; shade"[19]
- "to follow [a person] about secretly in order to keep watch over his movements"[20]
- "to shelter or protect"

The Psalms contain beautiful imagery depicting the "shadow of God" as our protection.

God's shadow hovering close is a comforting image. When we're wrongly accused, misunderstood, taken advantage of, unfairly judged, need to be defended, or simply need help, the presence of God hovers as our protection. Allow God's shadow to move in:

- close enough to hear His gentle whisper.
- near enough to see His hands work in ways far beyond your understanding.
- faithfully enough to give fresh air to breathe, and food to nourish your souls.
- familiar enough to recognize His goodness.
- protective in ways you may never recognize.

Take refuge and hide in His shade from the heat of daily life. Wrap yourself in the security of Isaiah 25:4: *You have been a defense for the helpless, a defense for the needy in his distress, a refuge from the storm, a shade from the heat; for the breath of the ruthless is like a rain storm against a wall.* In His shade you're secure.

Call out to Him today. Become aware of the shadow that is with us at all times.

Make It Personal

When are you most aware of the shadow of God?

Today I Bring Praise and Thanksgiving For

Justice Is Coming

Read Psalm 58

Key Verses: 58:6–7 *O God, shatter their teeth in their mouth; break out the fangs of the young lions, O Lord. Let them flow away like water that runs off; when he aims his arrows, let them be as headless shafts.*

Evil and wickedness invade our lives simply because we exist in this world. It can be unbearable to watch, especially when we strive to live by God's standards. Harder still might be exposing our private thoughts about apparent injustice — to put pen to paper and write a prayer asking God to give the wicked what they deserve.

But that's what David did in this psalm. The nation's leadership, prior to David becoming king, was evil and unjust. David hated the evil, injustice, deceit, corruption, and selfishness that led people to do as they pleased. As a result, he wrote this imprecatory psalm — a psalm that invokes judgment, calamity, or curses upon his enemies and those he perceived as enemies of God. David passionately wanted justice because innocent people were suffering. He didn't do any of the things described in the psalm; instead, he asked God to bring justice.

Maybe we haven't vented our anger the way David did. But do we privately ponder why it looks like those who try to do right are losing and evil appears to be winning?

We strive to live in an honest way, but every month there's barely enough to pay the bills. On the other hand, our neighbor, who verbally scoffs at God, has a new Mercedes and other luxurious material possessions. And wicked corporations, such as the porn industry, make millions. Does God care?

Trust the sovereignty of God. Hold fast to the hope that God won't permit wickedness to win in the end. Proverbs 14:14 tells us *faithless will be fully repaid for their ways, and the good rewarded for theirs* (NIV).

Remain steadfast in doing what God wants. John 3:20–21 tells us, *All who do evil hate the light and refuse to go near it for fear their sins will be exposed. But those who do what is right come to the light so others can see that they are doing what God wants* (NLT).

God's in control. Evil won't win. Justice is coming.

Make It Personal

In what area do you feel like giving up because evil and injustice appear to be winning?

Today I Bring Praise and Thanksgiving For

The Strength of God

Read Psalm 59

Key Verses: 59:16–17 *But as for me, I shall sing of Your strength; yes, I shall joyfully sing of Your lovingkindness in the morning, for You have been my stronghold and a refuge in the day of my distress. O my strength, I will sing praises to You.*

*A*re you weary? Is your physical body tired? Are you mentally exhausted and emotionally wiped out? If you said yes to any of these, you need the same strength that God gives geese.

Geese fly in a V-formation. Each goose flies slightly above the bird in front of him, creating an uplift so they can fly longer due to the reduction of wind resistance. When a lead goose gets tired, it rotates to the back of the formation. When a goose falls out of formation it feels the resistance of flying alone and gets back into formation where it can glide and draw energy. Additionally, flying in this formation helps the birds communicate and keep track of one another. They honk when they need to encourage one another. If a goose gets sick and goes down, two other geese go down and stay with the sick goose until it can rejoin the formation or dies.

If God gave knowledge and strength to geese, how much more will He provide us with the strength we need to live righteously? We are created in God's image, and when we place our trust in Him, we're adopted into His family. As His children, God knows that we need strength to:

- oppose worldly ideals.

- manage emotions that go haywire.

- resist the lies of the enemy.

- survive when we're suffering and don't know what to do.

- persevere through heartbreak.

- endure change and transition.

- refrain from sin

Isaiah 40:29–31 is encouragement for us as we fly towards the next chapter in our lives: *He gives strength to the weary, and to him who lacks might He increases power. Though youths grow weary and tired, and vigorous young men stumble badly, yet those who wait for the Lord will gain new strength; they will mount up with wings like eagles, they will run and not get tired, they will walk and not become weary.*

Geese or eagles — let's fly in the strength of God.

Make It Personal

Are you flying alone? How would your life look different if you applied these truths?

Today I Bring Praise and Thanksgiving For

An Illogical Request

Read Psalm 60

Key Verse: 60:11 *O give us help against the adversary, for deliverance by man is in vain.*

We may view it as an illogical or insane request: God told Gideon to decrease the size of his army before heading into battle. Decrease? Yes, and by a huge amount. In fact, Gideon was left to fight the battle with only 300 men, a ratio of one to 450 . . . in favor of the enemy. But Gideon obeyed God's command and even received confirmation through another man's dream.

First, Gideon worshipped the Lord, then he divided the 300 men into three groups, each soldier with a trumpet and a pitcher containing a torch. Gideon told his men to follow his example. They trudged into the night prepared for battle, just as God told them. The torches and the trumpet blasts caused so much panic in the dark of night that the enemy soldiers attacked each other!

Gideon's small army of 300 defeated an army of thousands, and God received all the glory. Man didn't do it — God did. Read this entire amazing story for yourself in Judges 7:1–25.

David also learned through personal experience about God's ability to bring victory. It's a theme throughout Psalms. In Psalm 108:12 David described man's help: *Give us aid against the enemy, for human help is worthless* (NIV). Worthless.

Our natural inclination is to run to others for help: friends, family, attorneys, counselors, stock brokers, bankers. God can and will utilize other people to help us, but God is the One who intercedes and negotiates on our behalf. When our battle is resolved, we can see that there's no other explanation except that God did it.

Sometimes God asks us to do that which appears illogical. But always God asks us to depend only on Him and trust Him with the outcome. We learn to trust God most through experiences that require something only He can do.

Make It Personal

Do you depend on others to bring you victory? Why or why not? When is it most difficult to fully trust in God?

Today I Bring Praise and Thanksgiving For

The Rock

Read Psalm 61

Key Verse: 61:2 *Lead me to the rock that is higher than I.*

Known as the "Little Town That Rocks," Black Mountain, North Carolina has a group of people who paint and distribute rocks throughout the town. These rocks can pop up anywhere — on the school playground, under a bush at the park, in between stones on a pathway, even on an outdoor table at a quaint restaurant. All the painted designs are creative and beautiful. Although some appear to be painted by children, others look like illustrations in a picture book. Not all the rocks have inspirational messages, but many of them do.

One person who found a rock posted this comment to social media: "I found a rock painted with *I am with you always – Matthew 28:20* and it put a smile on my face."

A rock with that kind of message could be exactly what we need for the moment. The perfect words we need to hear. We feel inspired, encouraged, and hopeful.

Regardless of where we live, God is our Rock. First Samuel 2:2 tells us, *There is no one holy like the Lord, indeed no one besides You, nor is there any rock like our God.*

We need our Rock when we're:

- overwhelmed with responsibilities
- uncertain about the future
- disrupted, despite our plans, and forced to be flexible

- worried about a young child's difficulties in school or an adult child's work conditions
- waiting for an evaluation from a doctor or supervisor

Let God's Word inspire, encourage, and fill you with fresh hope. Psalm 18:2 says, *The Lord is my rock and my fortress and my deliverer, my God, my rock, in whom I take refuge; my shield and the horn of my salvation, my stronghold.*

Try this today: Pick up a rock and use it as a visual reminder.

Make It Personal

What are your needs today? Is it difficult for you to turn to God, the Rock? Why or why not?

Today I Bring Praise and Thanksgiving For

Unshaken

Read Psalm 62

Key Verse: 62:6 *He only is my rock and my salvation, my stronghold; I shall not be shaken.*

When do you feel rattled or emotionally shaken? Our response to daily circumstances might induce aggravation, confusion, even exasperation. A change of plans or a bout of depression can shake our steadfast foundation.

Many Bible characters were shaken at some point for the purpose of training and commitment. Few suffered as Job did. Job left a lasting legacy of commitment to God. He was described as blameless, upright, and able to resist evil (Job 1:1).

During Job's painful season, he lost nearly everything. He cried out to God in his distress. He wept too. But he held fast to his faith in Almighty God and refused to turn against Him. He declared, *"He knows the way I take; when He has tried me, I shall come forth as gold"* (Job 23:10). And that statement proved true. At the end of Job's suffering, God faithfully restored twice as much as Job had lost (Job 42:10).

Job was unshaken by unimaginable difficulty. And it wasn't because he was exceptional. He didn't depend on his wealth, or his personal strength — those were stripped from him. Job 23:12 identifies the power that enabled Job to maintain his integrity and remain faithful to God: *I have not departed from the command of His lips; I have treasured the words of His mouth more than necessary food.*

Job treasured God's words more than life-sustaining food. Do we love God's words as much? Are we as dependent? Time spent with God enabled Job to draw strength from the One in whom He could trust. Although God allowed adversity to come into Job's life, Job remained unshaken.

Like Job, we can remain unshaken when surrounded by shakable circumstances. By spending time with God in prayer and Bible study, we learn about God's great love for us as individuals and His faithfulness to see us through adversity. Then when hard times come, the Word of God is food that sustains us.

Make It Personal

Do you treasure God's Word regardless of the circumstances or do you turn to God only when times are tough? Why or why not?

Today I Bring Praise and Thanksgiving For

Lasting Satisfaction

Read Psalm 63

Key Verse 63:1 *O God, You are my God; I shall seek You earnestly; my soul thirsts for You, my flesh yearns for You, in a dry and weary land where there is no water.*

I love to sit on my front porch with a big glass of sweet tea on a warm day or a hot cup of coffee on a cold one. Even better is when friends or family stop by and join me. The beverage quenches my thirst, and friends make me happy.

Still, the time spent on the porch is temporary refreshment. God is the only One who can satisfy our thirst and refresh our soul for eternity. Anything else we use to quench the desires of our heart is temporary. Ultimately, they fail and disappoint.

Research on happiness and satisfaction reveal that in America, for example, only thirty-three percent of people say they're happy. This data reflects similar surveys that only one in three people are happy or satisfied.[21]

Do you know anyone who, despite their personal success or wealth, is dissatisfied?

Seeking satisfaction in other people, ourselves, or things is dangerous and can lead to all kinds of emotional problems. People who depend on themselves for ultimate satisfaction either become victims or narcissists who boasts about self-sufficiency. They might also become critical of others or demand attention.

We were designed for more than temporary pleasure. Our soul was created to thirst for God. Without Him, there's a void. Jesus said in John 6:35, *I am the bread of life; he who comes to Me will not hunger, and he who believes in Me will never thirst.* We can try to find satisfaction in other people and places. But Jesus tells us in John 4:14, *Whoever drinks of the water that I will give him shall never thirst; but the water that I will give him will become in him a well of water springing up to eternal life.*

God will refresh our weary hearts and satisfy our searching souls. He will fill us to overflowing with living water. We drink of Your lasting refreshment.

Make It Personal

Are you dry? Are you thirsty for some kind of satisfaction? If no, why not? If yes, tell Jesus you want Him to give you living water that comes only with trusting Jesus.

Today I Bring Praise and Thanksgiving For

Protecting Our Minds

Read Psalm 64

Key Verses 64:1–2 *Hear my voice, O God, in my complaint; preserve my life from dread of the enemy. Hide me from the secret counsel of evildoers, from the tumult of those who do iniquity.*

*W*hen my husband sets out for a motorcycle ride on a beautiful day, he wears the necessary protective gear: boots, a jacket with armored plates, leather pants or long jeans, and gloves. He puts on his most important protection last — his helmet.

Whether it's a soldier on the battlefield, or a man on a motorcycle, a helmet protects the brain.

In this psalm, David pleaded with God to protect him from the effects of stress. Can you relate?

Since our minds are one of the devil's greatest playing fields, we need to suit up with our protective helmet. The devil initiates irrational thoughts and wrong perceptions. Sometimes he uses other people to deliver these blatant lies. Some of Satan's weapons are fear, self-pity discouragement, worthlessness, and confusion.

We need protection from the Enemy who wants to devour our mind. 2 Timothy 1:7 tells us, *God has not given us a spirit of fear, but of power and of love and of a sound mind* (NKJV). *Phroneo* is the Greek word for "sound mind" and refers to intelligence and right thinking. In other words, God gives us a well-balanced mind and the ability to draw sound conclusions.

The battle in our minds is real. Sometimes people say things that render us hopeless or confused. They talk in ways that make us feel "less than." Their inaccurate assessment of our abilities or the person they think we are can be compelling. A real fight ensues in our heads.

But take heart. Psalm 140:7 is a powerful defense: *O God the Lord, the strength of my salvation, You have covered my head in the day of battle.* David specifically asked God to shield his head.

When Jesus was being taunted and tempted by Satan, He spoke the Scriptures to fight against Satan's lie (Matthew 4:1–11).

We can't fight with a weapon we don't have. We protect our minds when we fill it with God's truth, which is found in God's Word.

Make It Personal

What steps will you take to protect your mind?

Today I Bring Praise and Thanksgiving For

Dwelling with God

Read Psalm 65

Key Verse: 65:4 *How blessed is the one whom You choose and bring near to You to dwell in Your courts.*

*I*n an informal survey, I once asked if dwelling with God was important. One hundred percent responded it was important. The concept, however, was ambiguous. What does dwelling with God entail? In the Hebrew, the word translated *dwell* means to sit with or remain.

The Bible teaches us what dwelling with God means:

- The Holy Spirit resides with those who trust in Jesus. First Corinthians 3:16 tells us, *Did you not know that you are a temple of God and that the Spirit of God dwells in you?* The Greek word translated "dwells" refers to a home or a permanent residence. Thus, God dwells with us wherever we go because He inhabits our hearts.

- God is an active participant in our daily business. We attempt to sit, spend time, and remain with Him. We casually sing praises and talk with Him while working. We schedule private time to pray. We make discovering His character a priority through devouring His words recorded in the Bible. Faith becomes active.

- Our attention is focused on what He is able to accomplish in and through our lives. With focused minds, we're less likely to become distracted by things that don't matter. Ephesians 3:20 tells us, *He is able to do far more abundantly beyond all that we ask or think, according to the power that works within us.*

- We seek God's direction. We'll make mistakes, but our desire is to do things God's way. John 14:26 tells us, *The Helper, the Holy Spirit . . . will teach you all things.*

- When our hearts are broken, He puts us back together. Isaiah 57:15 tells us, *I dwell on a high place . . . and also with the lowly of spirit in order to revive.*

- Supernatural strength enables us to behave in a Christ-like way. Ezekiel 37:27 reminds us, *My dwelling place also will be with them; and I will be their God, and they will be My people.* God is with us. Psalm 91:1 tells us, *He who dwells in the shelter of the Most High will abide in the shadow of the Almighty.*

Dwelling with God is one hundred percent a blessed life.

Make It Personal

Do you agree or disagree that dwelling with God is a blessing? Explain. In what ways do you desire to dwell?

Today I Bring Praise and Thanksgiving For

Refined

Read Psalm 66

Key Verse: 66:10 *You have refined us as silver is refined.*

efiners work with imperfect materials to create something beautiful. God is the original Refiner and He is creating something beautiful in us. Let's compare:

The Goldsmith/Silversmith	God
The refiners use rocks that have been squeezed under the earth's heat and pressure.	**Malachi 3:3** *He will sit as a smelter and purifier of silver, and He will purify the sons of Levi and refine them like gold and silver, so that they may present to the Lord offerings in righteousness.*
First, the rock is broken and then the precious metals are exposed to heat.	**Jeremiah 23:29** *Is not my word like fire, declares the Lord, and like a hammer which shatters a rock?*
The unrefined silver is placed in a crucible (a metal container) and heated to remove the dross. Gold is put in the furnace, then the dross removed.	**Proverbs 17:3** *The refining pot is for silver and the furnace for gold, but the Lord tests the heart.* **Isaiah 48:10** *See, I have refined you, though not as silver; I have tested you in the furnace of affliction.*

The dross continues to be removed until only the gold or silver remains. Each time it's refined, it becomes more precious.	**Proverbs 25:4** *Remove the dross from the silver and a silversmith can produce a vessel.* **Job 23:10** *He knows the way that I take; when he has tested me, I will come forth as gold.*
When the refiner looks into the silver and sees his reflection, the process is complete.	**Psalm 66:12** *We went through fire and water; but you brought us out to rich fulfillment.*
A natural diamond is also formed in heat and pressure. When the rock is crushed, a diamond can be extracted. It's inclusions (small imperfections), don't go away. They make the diamond unique.	**Psalm 139:14** *I will give thanks to You, for I am fearfully and wonderfully made.*

As God examines our hearts, our impurities are revealed. While we are in the furnace of affliction, God removes the impurities (dross), creating a beautiful vessel to be used. And like the silversmith who knows his work is complete when he sees his reflection in the silver, God will see His reflection in us.

Make It Personal

When have you felt the heat from the furnace of affliction? What dross do you believe is coming to the surface?

Today I Bring Praise and Thanksgiving For

The Perfect Judge

Read Psalm 67

Key Verse: 67:4 *Let the nations be glad and sing for joy; for You will judge the peoples with uprightness.*

One night I was praying with my then five-year-old son during our bedtime routine. I prayed our regular prayer, and always asked God to help my son be a good boy. When I finished, I reached down to kiss his cheek and cover him up.

To my surprise, he said, "Mom, I don't like praying anymore."

"Why not?"

"How would you like it if I asked God to make you a good mom?"

Sadness overwhelmed my heart. He felt unfairly judged a bad boy. A short discussion and an apology clarified my intention and motivation of my prayer.

Have you ever felt wrongly judged? Our society is quick to convict others without evidence. Too often, we make assumptions about people — what they're thinking or feeling. We judge someone as snooty, then discover the person is shy around new people.

This kind of misunderstanding or mistake can never happen with God as our judge. When He judges, He is fair and right. He will judge His children, the wicked, and those who do wrong to His children. God hasn't missed the evil deeds done throughout the world. Psalm 9:8 tells us, *He will judge the world in righteousness; He will execute judgment for the peoples with equity.*

To *judge* in Hebrew means to "defend, vindicate, plead, execute judgment." We mustn't believe that is our responsibility. The Bible tells us in Hebrews 10:30, *Vengeance is Mine, I will repay.* God will judge fairly, putting earthly judges to shame (Isaiah 40:23).

There's no confusion or misunderstanding with God. He is the perfect judge.

Make It Personal

Have you ever judged someone wrongly only to find out your assessment was false? If so, what did that teach you?

Today I Bring Praise and Thanksgiving For

A Father to the Fatherless

Read Psalm 68

Key Verse: 68:5 *A father of the fatherless and a judge for the widows, is God in His holy habitation.*

Do others see your dad's mannerisms in you? Do people say you look like your father? Or maybe you don't know your father well enough to say.

A child may not know his or her father for many reasons. One reason is divorce. Divorce affects fifty percent of families,[22] and seventy-five percent of these children live with their mothers.[23]

I was a child from a broken family.

When I was a teenager, my father lived 3,000 miles away. I visited him once a year, but even then, he was emotionally, mentally, and spiritually, absent. I knew what a decent father–daughter relationship should be like, but ours was void of depth or personal interest. I tried hard to be good so he'd like me, but that didn't close the gap between us.

Whether our fathers are absent physically or emotionally, we have a perfect Father in God. Isn't it amazing that the Creator of the Universe calls Himself our Father? When earthly fathers are not present, God says, *Leave your orphans behind, I will keep them alive; and let your widows trust in Me* (Jeremiah 49:11).

God will never abandon His children. He knows we need to be loved, protected, provided for, cherished, and valued. Our heavenly Father meets these needs when we call out to Him, whether or not we have an earthly father. God is also the perfect example of a father. He models love, faithfulness, trustworthiness, wisdom, kindness, forgiveness, and discipline. Although earthly fathers make mistakes, God never does.

After I finished college, my earthly father owned his mistake; he made things right with his family, and with God. A beautiful relationship began.

Regardless of our relationship with our biological, adoptive, or foster fathers, Ephesians 5:1 tells us, *Be imitators of God, as beloved children.* By embracing our heavenly Father's mannerisms, others will see our Father in us.

Make It Personal

When others look at you, do they see your heavenly Father? If you grew up without a good example for a father, in what ways is God a dad to you?

Today I Bring Praise and Thanksgiving For

Storms of Adversity

Read Psalm 69

Key Verses: 69:1–2 *Save me O God, for the waters have threatened my life. I have sunk in deep mire, and there is no foothold; I have come into deep waters, and a flood overflows me.*

*D*avid uses *mire* as a metaphor for pain and trouble . . . and here's a woman who can relate:

Her marriage dissolved on Monday and she was laid off from work on Tuesday. She packed up her belongings and moved out — into a storm of uncertainty and confusion. Along with her clothing, she packed financial devastation, failure, and guilt in her suitcase.

Deep waters. Storms. They have different names: trials, adversity, suffering, hardship. Regardless of the name we give them, storms knock us off our stable foundation and render us powerless. Everything we thought we knew suddenly becomes uncertain. We're whisked away by the winds of turmoil. Hailstones pound our hearts and minds.

Our struggle might be a hurricane-type storm with lasting consequences, changing the landscape of our circumstances. Or perhaps, our pain can be compared to a heavy rainstorm that keeps us inside all day. In other storms, we're drowning . . . gasping for air and wondering if we'll ever breathe fresh air again.

With His disciples in a boat on the Sea of Galilee, Jesus encountered a raging storm that ferociously shook the boat.

While Jesus slept, the disciples were gripped with fear. When they woke Jesus, He didn't get out of the boat to rescue Himself. He stayed with His beloved disciples in the vessel, then with power and authority, calmed the storm (Mark 4:35–41). Jesus stays with us in our storms too. He'll never abandon us.

Another time, while Jesus walked on water, He extended His hand to Peter and asked him to get out of the boat and come toward Him. Peter did. While he kept his eyes on Jesus, he walked on the surface of water. But when he looked away and saw the vastness of the wind and sea, he became afraid and began to sink (Matthew 14:28–30).

While sloshing through storms, refuse to look at the terrifying circumstances. Focus on Jesus. He's our shelter in the storm.

Make It Personal

Are you in the midst of a raging storm? If so, describe it. If not, reflect on a past storm. In what ways did Jesus meet your needs?

Today I Bring Praise and Thanksgiving For

Seeking God

Read Psalm 70

Key Verse: 70:4 *Let all who seek You rejoice and be glad in You.*

The Bible tells us in Luke 19:1-9 about a man named Zacchaeus. He was a short man who loved his wealth more than he loved people. After he heard Jesus was passing through town, he climbed a tree to get above the crowd so he could see Jesus. When Jesus walked through town, He wasn't surprised by a man in the tree. Jesus called Zacchaeus by name and told him to come down and spend time with Him.

Acts 8:25-39 tells us an Ethiopian official was also actively seeking, but wasn't sure what he needed. He wanted to know more about Judaism, so he read their Scriptures. God was working behind the scenes to answer the Ethiopian's questions. God told Phillip to go minister to the Ethiopian. Courageously, Phillip approached his chariot and then explained that the book of Isaiah was foreshadowing the Savior, Jesus. The Ethiopian instantly believed.

What is similar about the experiences of these two men? They both longed to know the Savior and went looking for Him. When He revealed Himself to them, they responded.

James 4:8 tells us, *Draw near to God and He will draw near to you.*

Jesus told Zacchaeus to come to Him *that day at that moment.* The Ethiopian was so excited to know God that when he saw a river he said he wanted to be baptized *at that moment.*

Isaiah 55:6–7 tells us, *Seek the Lord while He may be found; call upon Him while He is near.* These men did, and that decision changed their lives.

Have we done the same? If we have, then our actions will show we have. If we haven't, we can follow the examples of the Ethiopian and Zacchaeus. Let's not procrastinate any longer. When we seek God, we will find Him.

Make It Personal

In what ways do you seek the Savior? Where do you most often find Him?

Today I Bring Praise and Thanksgiving For

Beauty from Ashes

Read Psalm 71

Key Verse: 71:20 *Though You have made me see troubles, many and bitter, You will restore my life again; from the depths of the earth you will again bring me up.* (NIV)

Viewing the charred trees was a reminder of the trouble that had occurred.

I vividly recalled the sound of the fire engine sirens. Black smoke had impaired our view of the mountain ridge. When the smoke finally cleared and the fire was extinguished, we could see where the flames had licked the mountain ridge trees, stripping them of life.

Months later, I returned to the mountain hiking trail and stood amidst charred trees. I moved closer to touch a tree, and that's when I saw it — a tiny sprout of new life. A single, fresh branch with one tiny leaf. I smiled.

When we experience trouble in our lives, it can feel like flames of intense "heat" beating against our bodies, minds, and souls. Our situation stinks like the charred limbs on the trees. Confusion, like smoke, hinders our movement and impedes our thoughts.

But take heart. God tells us in Isaiah 43:2, *When you walk through the fire, you will not be scorched, nor will the flame burn you.* The *New Living Translation* says, *When you walk through the fire of oppression, you will not be burned up; the flames will not consume you.*

God brought new life to that charred tree. We aren't promised a trouble-free life. But we do have the promise in Isaiah 61:3 that God will *bestow on them a crown of beauty instead of ashes* (NIV).

God will bring new life to us as well — beauty from ashes.

Make It Personal

In what way can you relate to being burned? When have you felt that all you have left is charred remains? Do you see new life beginning? If yes, how so? If no, what do you think you need to do to experience new growth?

Today I Bring Praise and Thanksgiving For

Rule Your Castle

Read Psalm 72

Key Verse: 72:1 *Give the king Your judgements, O God, and Your righteousness to the king's son.*

There's some question about whether David or Solomon wrote this psalm. Whoever wrote this prayer, he asked God for wisdom to reign well. Parts of it are prophetic, referring to Jesus as the coming King.

We may not be ruling a kingdom as David or Solomon did. But we've been adopted into the family of the Highest King, making us princesses, entrusted with our castles — the place we call home.

This psalm is reflective of the responsibilities each of us face and the wisdom we need. For our castles to operate smoothly, we need what Proverbs 2 tells us in verses 10–11: *Wisdom will enter your heart and knowledge will be pleasant to your soul; discretion will guard you, understanding will watch over you.*

Judging the motivation of quarreling children requires astute perception. Discerning between a truth and a lie requires a high degree of wisdom. Knowing which TV programs, books, or friends, foster a pattern of right thinking can be exhausting. Confronting teachers, coaches, or another parent to vindicate your child may backfire. We care for those who live within our castle, with compassion. Forgiveness is packed along with the lunch each day. Providing nutrition for their bodies and food for their soul is a daily responsibility.

When those in our castle are injured, we place Band Aids on knees, offer cookies and milk, or sit with a teen struggling with a deteriorating relationship. As leaders of the castle, we wipe their tears. We want to rescue our children from pain, but that's not always possible.

For some, your castle is an office or a retail store. Your daily work requires similar responsibilities. Dealing with combative, backstabbing, argumentative employees requires wisdom. Those competing for advancement can steal your energy.

Let's lift the words "lick the dust" (v. 9) off the page as a reminder that, with God's help, our enemies will be defeated. Write this verse down and tape it to the refrigerator.

God entrusts us with important work within our castle and kingdom. He has also provided what we need to rule effectively: the Bible — our textbook, and the Holy Spirit — our teacher (John 14:26). Treasure both.

Make It Personal

What do you consider to be the most complicated part of ruling your castle?

Today I Bring Praise and Thanksgiving For

Strength Training

Read Psalm 73

Key Verse: 73:26 *My flesh and my heart may fail, but God is the strength of my heart and my portion forever.*

Needing a break from the numbing work of sitting in front of a computer all day, I pulled on my exercise clothes and headed to the nearby fitness center. It was crowded as usual with people of different sizes, shapes, and ages, each with varying abilities and goals. Some were doing resistance training with bands. Others were lifting heavy weights to build strong muscles. A few were running on treadmills, attempting to raise their heart rates. Swimmers were doing laps, building endurance. But regardless of their activity, everyone had one thing in common: they were all exercising their physical bodies and strengthening their muscles.

Strengthening our bodies is important and contributes to a good quality of life. But we also need to be strengthened spiritually. By spending time in God's Word, we receive strength training in the following areas:

- Resistance. James 4:7 tells us, *Submit therefore to God. Resist the devil and he will flee from you.* The power of the Holy Spirit enables us to resist crossing the border into sin.

- Strength. Ephesians 6:10 tells us, *Be strong in the Lord and in the strength of His might.* Our strength comes from God, not from self-reliance.

151

- Endurance. Hebrews 12:1 tells us, *Lay aside every encumbrance and the sin which so easily entangles us, and let us run with endurance.* If God provides the willpower, we'll be less likely to give up or back down. Endurance enables us to stay on course.

- Perseverance. Galatians 6:9 tells us, *Let us not lose heart in doing good, for in due time we will reap if we do not grow weary.* Lifting weights one time will not produce the desired effect. Only with perseverance will we reach our goal.

No matter who we are, where we've come from, or where we're going, we need to work out in the gym of spiritual growth. Through prayer and Bible reading, God will show us the best way to get on track and stay there.

As a physical workout brings a better quality of life, a spiritual workout brings a victorious life.

Make It Personal

Have you been in the spiritual gym lately? If not, what adjustments can you make to get that workout on your schedule?

Today I Bring Praise and Thanksgiving For

Never Destroyed

Read Psalm 74

Key Verses: 74:7–8 *They have burned Your sanctuary to the ground; They have defiled the dwelling place of Your name. They said in their heart, "Let us completely subdue them." They have burned all the meeting places of God in the land.*

The Babylonians had destroyed the temple — the place where God's presence dwelled. They created chaos wherever they went and laughed at all the evil they had done. God's people traveled many miles to worship in the temple. So the writer of this psalm (Asaph) called out to God and asked Him why He wouldn't respond and defend his people.

History repeats itself. Wickedness runs rampant and sin is glorified in our world today. We call out to God in the same way Asaph did. God didn't miss a thing then, and He doesn't ignore us now. When the Babylonians destroyed the temple, it appeared that wickedness was winning. But ultimately, they were conquered by the Medes and Persians. Likewise, those who do evil and blatantly blaspheme God aren't going to win today. God remains on the throne.

Those who rebel against God can only destroy a shell — a temporary building or covering, or even a body. They can never destroy what is eternal. In 2 Corinthians 4:8–9 Paul wrote, *We are afflicted in every way, but not crushed; perplexed, but not despairing; persecuted, but not forsaken; struck down, but not destroyed.*

What an encouraging truth! Hardships may come and evil may invade, but we'll never be destroyed. How would you fill in the blanks?

I am afflicted with _____, but not crushed.
I'm perplexed about _____, but not despairing.
I'm persecuted because of _____, but not forsaken.
I am temporarily struck down by _____, but I will never, ever, be destroyed.

Destruction is around us but never within us. No one can take away God's presence. They may take our bodies — the outside shell. But never can anyone take the internal — our faith and our God. In this way, we can never be destroyed.

Make It Personal

Is there any area in your life in which you feel destroyed? How are you encouraged by today's verses?

Today I Bring Praise and Thanksgiving For

God's Perfect Timing

Read Psalm 75

Key Verse: 75:2 *When I select an appointed time, it is I who judge with equity.*

*H*ave you ever asked God, "Why are You taking so long? Don't you care?"

Timing is defined as "the ability to select the precise moment for doing something for optimum effect." In Esther's story, timing was the decisive factor in whether a group of people would survive or be annihilated.

Esther, a Jewish orphan, was raised by her cousin Mordechai. When she was a teenager she was chosen to appear before the king in a beauty contest. The winner would become queen. Fearing prejudice might prevent her from becoming queen, Esther kept her Jewish heritage a secret. For the next year, she took part in beauty treatments while she waited her turn to go before the king. When Esther went before King Ahasuerus (King Xerxes), she found favor with him and he crowned her queen.

Later, a man named Haman, rose to such power that officials knelt before him to show respect. But Mordechai refused to bow to anyone except God and this infuriated Haman. Haman knew Mordechai was a Jew and wanted to kill every Jew in the kingdom. Mordechai asked Esther to use her influence as queen and beg the king for mercy for the Jewish people. Esther had a choice — be scared or be obedient.

Because the day of death for the Jews was still eleven months away, she could have waited. But Mordechai said she had become queen *for such a time as this* (Esther 4:14). In other words, don't procrastinate. Esther approached the king and requested that he spare her and her people's lives. The king was outraged at Haman's plot. Haman was hanged and the Jewish people were saved (Esther chapters 1-10).

At exactly the right time, God used Esther to accomplish His plans. Trust that God's timing is perfect and believe He is working behind the scenes for you just as He was for Esther.

Make It Personal

What is the hardest part about waiting for God's perfect timing in your current situation?

Today I Bring Praise and Thanksgiving For

Get Dressed

Read Psalm 76

Key Verse: 76:3 *There He broke the flaming arrows, the shield and the sword and the weapons of war.*

The psalms are full of battles: spiritual, emotional, and physical ones. Battles are a part of our daily life too (John 16:33). Which of these battles are you facing?

Depression	Defeat	Hopelessness	Unworthiness
Unloved	Fear	Insecurity	Stress
Disappointment	Worry	Dissatisfaction	Confusion
Exhaustion	Anger	Guilt/shame	Stuck/paralysis
Arrogance	Pride	Independence	Temptation

God equipped us with armor to fight our battles. Ephesians 6:11 tells us, *Put on the full armor of God, so that you will be able to stand firm against the schemes of the devil.*

Our armor is described in Ephesians 6:14–17: *Stand firm therefore, having girded your loins with truth, and having put on the breastplate of righteousness, and having shod your feet with the preparation of the gospel of peace; in addition to all, taking up the shield of faith with which you will be able to extinguish all the flaming arrows of the evil one. And take the helmet of salvation, and the sword of the spirit, which is the word of God.*

157

The armor is identified in bold and means:

- **Girded with truth**: The truth of God's Word encircles us and holds us together.
- **Breastplate of righteousness**: The breastplate is worn in battle to protect our heart and vital organs. The apostle Paul tells us to protect our heart and soul.
- **Feet shod in preparation**: Satan will attack, so be ever vigilant.
- **Shield of faith**: When Satan attacks, our faith acts as a shield to deflect the flaming arrows of the devil.
- **Helmet of salvation**: The helmet protects our thoughts. The assurance of our salvation is our defense against anything Satan throws at us.
- **Sword of the Spirit**: The sword is an offensive weapon. We use God's Word to counter-attack Satan's lies.

Hebrews 4:12 tells us, *The word of God is living and active and sharper than any two-edged sword.* God's Word is what we use to fight every battle we face. Suit up and defeat the enemy's attacks. Today, we dress for battle!

Make It Personal

Is part of your spiritual wardrobe missing? If so, which part?

Today I Bring Praise and Thanksgiving For

Sleeplessness

Read Psalm 77

Key Verse: 77:2 *In the day of my trouble I sought the Lord; in the night my hand was stretched out without weariness; my soul refused to be comforted.*

Years ago, our family went through a difficult season, and I found it difficult to sleep. One night in particular, I was worried, scared, and confused — a perfect combination for another sleepless night. After tossing and turning a while, I got up and turned on the television. The news was all bad, so I turned it off. Sitting on the bed, I switched on the light on the side table. Weary from crying, I whispered, "God, help."

Hoping to find encouragement, I opened the side table drawer and shuffled through the items in it. At the bottom of the drawer was a wrinkled page from a magazine. On it were the words of Psalm 62:5: *My soul, find rest in God; my hope comes from Him.* I smiled. Focused on that truth, I turned off the light and went to sleep.

Recent research identified anxiety, stress, and depression as some of the most common causes of insomnia.[24] Are you dealing with trouble and anxiety that leads to sleeplessness?

Reading Scripture isn't an instant solution — the problems will still be there when you wake up. But reading the Bible brings peace; we're reminded to put our hope in God. Why not write the following verses on sticky notes and leave them beside the bed so you can read them before drifting off to sleep?

- Psalm 29:11 *The Lord will bless His people with peace.*
- Psalm 4:8 *In peace I will both lie down and sleep, for You alone, O Lord, make me to dwell in safety.*
- Psalm 127:2 *He gives to His beloved sleep* (ESV).
- Matthew 11:28 *Come to Me, all who are weary and heavy-laden, and I will give you rest.*

You can also do what my mother did — she slept with her Bible. So sleep. Then wake up refreshed and ready for a new day. And if our problems still linger, we can start the nighttime routine all over again.

Make It Personal

What keeps you up at night? What helps you sleep well?

Today I Bring Praise and Thanksgiving For

A Life of Integrity

Read Psalm 78

Key Verse: 78:72 *He shepherded them according to the integrity of his heart, and guided them with his skillful hands.*

The Bible gives many examples of people who lived with integrity. Integrity is defined as being honest and having strong moral principles. If we're going to impact other people in a positive way, it's imperative that we conduct ourselves in this way.

Deborah, a prophetess and judge, is an example of a woman whose integrity impacted a generation of people. During Israel's oppression, she led with integrity and extraordinary wisdom. Deborah told Barak to take 10,000 soldiers into battle against the Canaanites and promised that God would give them victory. When Barak insisted that Deborah come with him, she said, *I will surely go with you; nevertheless, the honor shall not be yours on the journey that you are about to take, for the Lord will sell Sisera* [the Canaanite commander] *into the hands of a woman* (Judges 4:9). Barak's army killed all of Sisera's men (Judges 4:16). Sisera fled but was killed by a woman, Jael (Judges 4:21).

Deborah listened to God and humbly submitted to His will. She called the people to battle, led them out of idolatry, and restored Israel's dignity. As a result, the nation enjoyed peace for forty years.

We may not be in a leadership position like Deborah, but we do have the opportunity to show integrity in our homes, churches, work places, and communities. We can inspire those within our sphere of influence to live a life of integrity too.

Maybe you've heard that "integrity is doing what's right when no one is looking." Every challenge, difficulty, or experience is an opportunity to develop character. The lessons learned guide us towards integrity. We can show integrity in big and small ways. We can:

- keep our word.
- refuse to embellish the truth.
- decide what is right or wrong based on God's Word.
- respect God, ourselves, and others.
- be sincere, honest, and authentic.

The Bible tells us in Philippians 1:27, *Conduct yourselves in a manner worthy of the gospel of Christ.* Christians — Christ followers — are called to live with integrity. Deborah's relationship with God enabled her to live with integrity. And ours can too.

Make It Personal

How can you teach the next generation to live in integrity?

Today I Bring Praise and Thanksgiving For

Jealous for You

Read Psalm 79

Key Verse: 79:5 *How long, O Lord? Will You be angry forever? Will Your jealousy burn like fire?*

God was faithful to His people and freed them from their bondage in Egypt. On countless occasions He showed up in astonishing ways and provided for their needs. Miracles were frequent, yet the people continued to rebel. Oh, they obeyed God and enjoyed His blessings for a short time, but then they'd go right back to doing what they desired, living for themselves in rebellion towards God.

It became a vicious cycle. The sins of generations mounted, so God poured out His wrath.

Asaph, the writer of this psalm, admitted the nation's wrong-doing and questioned God: *Will You be angry forever?* Then he said something that may surprise us — will Your jealousy continue? We might be surprised by the verbiage and wonder how a sinless God can be jealous — a behavior that Galatians 5:20 calls sin.

God is further identified as a jealous God in Exodus 20:4–5: *You shall not make for yourself an idol, or any likeness of what is in heaven above or on the earth beneath or in the water under the earth. You shall not worship them or serve them; for I, the Lord Your God, am a jealous God, visiting the iniquity of the fathers on the children, on the third and the fourth generations of those who hate Me.* Exodus 34:14 reiterates, *You shall not worship any other god, for the*

Lord, whose name is Jealous, is a jealous God.

Despite God's command, the people made idols and worshiped them instead of giving their worship to God. God is jealous for what already belongs to Him — His people and His worship. He can't share His glory with another. He is jealous for us! When we make other things more important than God, His jealousy burns because He wants us back. He loves us that much.

A lack of devotion for God makes Him jealous for us. God is worthy of our loyalty. Let's give Him our all today.

Make It Personal

Have you given God any reason to be jealous for you? If yes, describe the competition.

Today I Bring Praise and Thanksgiving For

Reflecting His Light

Read Psalm 80

Key Verse: 80:3 *O God, restore us and cause Your face to shine upon us, and we will be saved.*

On its own, the moon is dark 24/7; it generates no light. But when the moon reflects the sun, it shines brightly because it reflects the light from the sun.

Likewise, when God shines on us we're able to reflect the light of God and shine in a dark world.

We live in a dark world because of sin. The good news, however, is found in 1 John 1:5: *This is the message we have heard from Him and announce to you, that God is Light, and in Him there is no darkness at all.*

We need the light.

- The light becomes a lantern illuminating our fog-covered path so we know which way to go. (Psalm 119:105)

- The light resembles a flickering candle that takes away our fear. (Psalm 27:1)

- The light shines like a flashlight on our sinful habits and behaviors, revealing that which is harmful (Acts 26:18).

- In fact, the light is Jesus Christ. (John 9:5)

The phrase "cause Your face to shine upon us" is repeated three times in this psalm. What would make God's face shine on us? Consider how a parent looks with pleasure at her child because she's delighted with her child's choices, habits, and obedience. The child reciprocates and looks to her parent when seeking guidance and direction.

God is our faithful parent — our heavenly Father. He looks upon us favorably when we choose to live in obedience to Him. We still live in a sinful, dark world, but when our relationship is right with God, His light eclipses the darkness. Then we can do as Matthew 5:16 says, *Let your light shine before men in such a way that they may see your good works and glorify your Father who is in heaven.*

We shine because God shines *on* and *in* us. In Psalm 18:28 we read, *You light my lamp; the Lord my God illumines my darkness.*

A victorious existence is a life that shines.

Make It Personal

Do you feel overwhelmed by darkness? How so? When do you feel you are best able to shine? In what area do you most need a light?

Today I Bring Praise and Thanksgiving For

Speak, Lord

Read Psalm 81

Key Verse: 81:13 *Oh that My people would listen to Me.*

The game was tied and the bases were loaded. Will's team got up to bat. As soon as Will's teammate hit the ball, every coach from both teams began yelling orders:

"Run here!"

"Throw the ball to first!"

"Run to third!"

"Go home!"

Parents were cheering, clapping, and shouting too. The game was organized confusion and mayhem. I wondered, *How do these boys know what to do with everyone screaming directions? They must be trained to focus only on their coach's voice.*

We, too, have many voices shouting at us. We need to train our ears to identify God's whispers. John 10:4 tells us, *The sheep follow Him because they know His voice.*

Discerning truth is difficult when we're bombarded with lies. For example, the devil uses social media, secular magazines, and television to suggest we must look a certain way or be a specific size. He also uses these same resources to imply we're not smart enough, gifted enough, or good enough. Television suggests that adultery and scandals bring satisfaction and self-fulfillment. The lifestyles of Hollywood celebrities and other famous people, can make us dissatisfied with our lives. The media portrays selfishness as admirable and filthy conversations as the norm. Sin is exalted. If we don't accept that viewpoint, we may feel something is wrong with us.

It is imperative that we combat these lies with God's truth. John 16:7–8 tells us that God sent a helper — an advocate and counselor known as the Holy Spirit — to help us discern truth.

The truth is found in the Bible; the primary tool the Holy Spirit uses to guide us toward truth. Billy Graham once said, "One can approach the Bible with a cold, rationalistic attitude, or one can do so with reverence and the desire to hear God speak."[25]

Let's turn off the noise of our culture and turn on time with God. Just as Will and his teammates had to identify their coach's voice, we must identify our coach's voice.

Make It Personal

Whose voice have you been listening to?

Today I Bring Praise and Thanksgiving For

An Understanding Heart

Read Psalm 82

Key Verse: 82:5 *They do not know nor do they understand; they walk about in darkness.*

They weren't like him.

God gave the earthly judges the responsibility of applying His law fairly, using a discerning spirit and seeking wisdom from God. But many failed to uphold God's moral law. This psalm is an account of God judging the wicked judges. They weren't like Solomon.

When Solomon first became king, he prayed, *Give Your servant an understanding heart to judge Your people to discern between good and evil* (1 Kings 3:9). Solomon ruled well and depended on God for success. For example, on one occasion, two women came to him. Each claimed that a live baby belonged to her and a dead baby was the other woman's. Solomon used remarkable God-given wisdom to discern the truth and justice was done (1 Kings 3:16-28). But note what the people said: *When all Israel heard of the judgment which the king had handed down, they feared the king, for they saw that the wisdom of God was in him to administer justice* (v. 28). They saw God in Solomon.

Today, we may not be in the position to judge or rule over people like Solomon. But we regularly make decisions. Like Solomon, we're servants of God — as Solomon identified himself. As such, we are charged with pointing others to God by our actions, and we're in need of an understanding heart and mind to interact with all kinds of people. In Psalm 119:34 we read, *Give me understanding, that I may observe Your law and keep it with all my heart.* Psalm 119:66 says, *Teach me good discernment and knowledge.* This doesn't happen naturally. Truth, discernment, and knowledge come from knowing God and listening to Him.

A good example of a time to have an understanding heart is dealing with our children. Each one is unique and needs to be trained and disciplined in ways that effectively meet their needs.

Whether it's disciplining and guiding our children, cooperating with co-workers, or cultivating relationships, Proverbs 3:5 reminds us, *Trust in the Lord with all your heart and do not lean on your own understanding.*

When we ask Him, God gives each of us the ability to discern the right thing to do. Then, like Solomon, onlookers will see God directing us.

Make It Personal

In what area of your life are you seeking to understand?

Today I Bring Praise and Thanksgiving For

True Humility

Read Psalm 83

Key Verse: 83:2 *Behold, Your enemies make an uproar, and those who hate You have exalted themselves.*

She took a risk. Sitting at Jesus's feet was not appropriate behavior for a woman. But that wasn't at the forefront of Mary's mind. Driven by a heart full of gratitude, she poured expensive perfume on His feet and dried them with her hair. (John 12:3)

To those present, it appeared that Mary wasted perfume worth a year's wages. And she was behaving improperly by letting down her hair in public, which was not permissible for Jewish woman. Mary humbled herself before the Lord and her courageous act was recorded in the Bible. Recognizing Jesus was the Savior of the world, she saw her unworthiness to be in His holy presence. In humility, she loved and worshipped Jesus.

In the context of this psalm, the writer begs God to confront His enemies, who he identifies with various verbs that express their hatred towards God. Exalting themselves is one of these. To *exalt* means "to raise in rank, power, or character." A synonym is "to applaud" oneself. The enemies of God were proud and hateful. But Mary showed love for Jesus by her humility.

The Bible tells us in 1 Peter 5:6, *Humble yourselves under the mighty hand of God, that He may exalt you at the proper time.* Humility doesn't mean we have a low opinion of ourselves. Neither does it deny one's knowledge or level of education.

171

Humility doesn't mean that we allow others to advance over us. Proverbs 11:2 tells us, *When pride comes, then comes dishonor, but with the humble is wisdom.* Wisdom, knowledge, and confidence in God inspire an attitude of humility.

Humility is giving God credit when He works through us. Humility is an attitude of submission to God's will for our lives. We strive to please Him — not to seek the admiration of others.

Using our talents, being called an outstanding citizen, honored with awards, chosen as employee/person of the year, are all excellent. But what we do with our lives or what we become is because God made it possible. In gratitude and thanksgiving to God for our accomplishments, we show true humility.

Make It Personal

Is there any area in your life in which you haven't given God credit?

Today I Bring Praise and Thanksgiving For

Pools of Blessings

Read Psalm 84

Key Verse: 84:6 *Passing through the valley of Baca they make it a spring; the early rain also covers it with blessings.*

For a brief time, my walk-in closet became my refuge — a shelter from the storm. In solitude and darkness, I spilled my thoughts out to God. Tears were the other thing that spilled. Lots of them. I referred to my space as my puddle of tears.

During our lifetime, we will experience many seasons. Some will be painful; others joyful. All of them can be meaningful seasons when we allow God to teach us, even if they bring tears.

In most Bible translations, the Hebrew word *Baca* is used in verse six. Baca means weeping or lamenting. It refers to a balsam tree whose sap oozes like tears. The *New Living Translation* uses language we can better understand: Valley of Weeping.

When overwhelmed with sadness, some may briefly shed a tear; others may weep for long periods of time. Eyelids swell. Vision blurs. Our nostrils cannot take in air. Sometimes heartache fills our soul to the point we can longer feel other emotions. We avoid other activities so we can crawl under the blanket of seclusion and isolation — or a coat in the closet. An overpowering sense of exhaustion engulfs us.

For other people, crying actual tears are difficult. But their heart is crying tears of pain as it breaks.

God sees our tears. He pays attention to our weeping in the night. He also hears the silence when we're numb.

Psalm 30:5 tells us, *Weeping may last for the night, but a shout of joy comes in the morning.*

God is faithful to His promises. We may be in a season of weeping and mourning and create a puddle of tears in our private place. But these tears — this puddle — will become a pool of blessing.

Make It Personal

Are you in or have you been through the Valley of Baca? What blessings do you receive? What blessings do you anticipate?

Today I Bring Praise and Thanksgiving For

Restored

Read Psalm 85

Key Verse: 85:4 *Restore us, O God of our salvation.*

Many of us watch home improvement, fixer-upper type shows. It's exciting to witness an old, dilapidated home come back to life. New paint brightens the rooms. Space is used in creative and innovative ways. Worn-out floors are stripped of old paint and then new stain makes them shine again.

Sometimes renovators use discarded lumber to construct something new. In one episode I watched, lumber from a broken-down barn was used to construct a large, family-style, kitchen table, stained and polished with a variety of shades of brown. Not only was the table useful, but it was also symbolic of something once loved.

Sometimes we mentally, emotionally, and spiritually feel like an old, worn-down piece of wood flooring stomped on many times. Too much furniture has been dragged across us. We need to be restored. Like the wood floors, we need to take off the old and put on the new.

Colossians 3:8–9 tells us what to take off: *But now you also, put them all aside: anger, wrath, malice, slander, and abusive speech from your mouth. Do not lie to one another, since you laid aside the old self with its evil practices.*

Off with the old to put on the new. Colossians 3:12-14 tells us what to put on: *A heart of compassion, kindness, humility, gentleness and patience; bearing with one another, and forgiving each other . . . put on love.*

We don't do this on our own. Second Corinthians 5:17 tell us, *Therefore if anyone is in Christ, he is a new creature; the old things passed away; behold, new things have come.* Christ living in us makes us new.

There's more. Jesus Christ gives us a second chance, fresh joy, newfound strength, and a renewed spirit.

Every day we're offered God's love, kindness, compassion, and faithfulness. His constant care makes us new. Sweet transformation. Not once a year, but as often as we need it.

Let's ask God to restore our minds and attitudes, our families and marriages, our work, our hopes and dreams. Then, we'll shine like new wood floors and brighten any room.

Make It Personal

What area in your life needs the most restoration?

Today I Bring Praise and Thanksgiving For

When I Get Angry

Read Psalm 86

Key Verse: 86:15 *You, O Lord, are a God merciful and gracious, slow to anger and abundant in lovingkindness and truth.*

The eight-year-old looked up at me from his schoolwork. Without provocation he said, "I get mad easy."

"What makes you angry?" I asked.

"When someone gets in my face or in my bubble. I get mad if someone forgets my birthday too."

I was surprised by both this innocent child's honest expression and the way he clearly articulated his anger and its triggers.

"My mom says I have to say I'm sorry when I get mad at people," he continued.

Can you relate to this child? *Anger* is defined as "a strong feeling of displeasure and usually of antagonism." Anger is a God-given emotion. Used at the right time, anger can be an appropriate response. In our key verse's description of God, we're shown that God's anger comes slowly. Exodus 34:6 also reveals that God becomes angry — but He's slow in doing so. Sometimes we're legitimately aroused to anger because of the deception and injustice in our communities or because God's laws are mocked. With righteous anger, we take a stand against injustice.

On the other hand, unjustified anger — anger that hasn't been dealt with, or lingering anger that festers — can become a tool the devil uses to defeat us. Proverbs 14:17 tells us that *a quick-tempered man acts foolishly*. Anger that flares quickly can lead to fragmented families, destruction of a person's mental and/or physical health, and shatter personal dreams.

When we're slow to anger, we model the patience of God. The "waiting time" before anger erupts, is an opportunity to seek out the offender's motivation. James 1:20 advises us to be *slow to anger; for the anger of man does not achieve the righteousness of God.*

If we're like this eight-year-old child who's easily angered, there is hope. God understands our frustration and will help us learn to deal with anger appropriately.

Make It Personal

What strategies do you use to keep anger at bay? What, if anything, is raising anger issues for you today?

Today I Bring Praise and Thanksgiving For

Springs of Joy

Read Psalm 87

Key Verse: 87:7 *All my springs of joy are in you.*

*W*ater sustains life.

Psalm 42:1 tells us, *As a deer pants for flowing streams, so pants my soul for you, O God* (ESV). Where God is, there is a life-sustaining stream of refreshment and joy. But many pursue joy in possessions, other people, or pleasure. One article I once read listed forty ways to discover joy. God was number forty on the list. The thirty-nine suggestions placed before God, were primarily tangible, temporary joys. Ultimately, this false joy results in sorrow and separation from God.

The Hebrew word for *spring* is *maqor*, meaning "fountain or wellspring." God said in Jeremiah 2:13, *They have forsaken Me, the fountain of living waters, to hew for themselves cisterns, broken cisterns that can hold no water.*

The joy found in the Lord, however, flows like a fountain. Nehemiah 8:10, reminds us, *Do not be grieved, for the joy of the Lord is your strength.* Wading in hardship may be difficult but it doesn't have to be joyless. Streams of joy can smooth the rocks in our path.

Romans 15:13 tells us, *Now may the God of hope fill you with all joy and peace in believing, so that you will abound in hope by the power of the Holy Spirit.* Joy comes with believing God and trusting His Word. Whether we're seeking joy for the first time or longing to rediscover it, we can:

- Study God's Word. Joy is a fruit of the Spirit and will naturally emerge when we're grounded in His Word.
- Pray for God to restore our joy, (Psalm 51:12)
- Observe nature and appreciate God's amazing creativity.
- Remember that salvation is the greatest gift, and we have eternal life with Him.

Find joy by coming to God's spring, where water continually moves — flowing over rocks and making the hard places smooth.

Make It Personal

Have you ever felt joyless? If so, how do these Scriptures encourage you?

Today I Bring Praise and Thanksgiving For

The Case for Morning

Read Psalm 88

Key Verse: 88:13 *But I, O Lord, have cried out to You for help, and in the morning my prayer comes before You.*

The sound of dozens of birds chirping rhythmically wake me. If my window is slightly raised, spring mornings provide a natural alarm clock. A ray of sun soon streams through the tiny arched window. The darkness disappears and a new day emerges.

With each morning comes hope and direction.

- Chirping birds serve as an alarm clock, reminding us of a rooster who also awakens the dawn. Jesus told Peter, *Truly I say to you that this very night, before a rooster crows, you will deny Me three times* (Matthew 26:34). May this remind us to deny ourselves, not Jesus. Jesus said in Matthew 16:24, *If anyone wishes to come after Me, he must deny himself, and take up his cross and follow Me.* By denying ourselves, we put away our selfish desires and seek God.

- Night ends as the sun arises. Darkness also symbolizes hardship. The writer of this psalm was depleted and miserable. He felt forsaken. Lamentations 3:22-24 tells us, *The Lord's lovingkindnesses indeed never cease, for His compassions never fail. They are new every morning; great is Your faithfulness. "The Lord is my portion," says my soul, "therefore I have hope in Him."*

- Scientists estimate the earth's age in millions of years, Bible scholars around 6,000 years. Either way, God has never forgotten to bring the morning. Each morning is a reminder of His faithfulness.

- God's help is available daily. Let's not ignore the guilt in our heart that leads to repentance so that help can begin.

- Mark 1:35 tells us that *in the early morning, while it was still dark, Jesus got up, left the house, and went away to a secluded place, and was praying there.* Jesus started his day with prayer that fueled His hope and direction.

Morning is a perfect time to reflect on God's faithfulness and embrace His will, help, and mercy as the new day begins.

Make It Personal

How will you deny yourself today?

Today I Bring Praise and Thanksgiving For

Walking with God

Read Psalm 89

Key Verse: 89:15 *How blessed is everyone who fears the Lord, who walks in His ways.*

I weighed myself and discovered I had gained five pounds in four months. Too many distractions and a busy schedule prevented me from being aware of what my body was taking in. The end result was an unpleasant change. I wasn't where I wanted to be.

Waking with God is similar. We must be diligent about spending time with God each day. When what we take in is void of God, unpleasant changes occur. We're not where we should be.

For many, the concept of "walking with God" is baffling. What does that even mean?

Simply defined, *walking* is a verb indicating a continuous movement; to move along; advance by steps. Micah 6:8 tells us, *What does the Lord require of you? To act justly and to love mercy and to walk humbly with your God* (NIV).

To walk with God means continuous movement in which every day is progress forward, or a step in the right direction, to getting to know the character of God. It's not only about the spiritual highs and happy moments we experience. It's more about the daily change, growth, and renewal that occur when we spend time with God. It's amazing to feel the grip of intimacy that begins to take place.

Walk also describes a manner of living — a lifestyle. Colossians 1:10 tells us, *Walk in a manner worthy of the Lord, to please Him in all respects, bearing fruit in every good work and increasing in the knowledge of God.*

Our daily encounters with God will not only open our eyes to see how God wants us to live, but we'll see that God is the strength and power that enables us to live this way. Walking in this manner transforms us and we begin to bear beautiful fruit.

Galatians 5:22-23 describes the progress we (and others) see: *The fruit of the Spirit is love, joy, peace, patience, kindness, goodness, faithfulness, gentleness, self-control.*

Keep the pace. Let's enjoy the beauty of a single day as we take steps closer to God.

Make It Personal

Are you getting your walk in each day? If yes, what are you learning? If no, what can you do to make time for a "walk" in your busy schedule?

Today I Bring Praise and Thanksgiving For

Hiding in Your Pocket

Read Psalm 90

Key Verse: 90:8 *You have placed our iniquities before You, our secret sins in the light of Your presence.*

In first grade, my son became interested in trading cards. To make sure he didn't take cards or other toys to school (per the school's policy), I habitually checked his backpack and pockets for stowaways.

After he passed the card and toy test one day, I drove him to school. When I picked him up, though, he was showing his cards to a teacher. I said, "I checked your backpack and coat pockets, and you didn't have those when you left home this morning. Eyes downcast, he mumbled, "You didn't check my underwear." Envision the subsequent morning — a full body search!

Sometimes children hide things from their parents. Do we also hide sin from our heavenly Father? Maybe these sins are less obvious than those mentioned in the Ten Commandments. Perhaps we inadvertently hide them because we haven't admitted them to ourselves. Denial, justification, and defensiveness are reasons we may not recognize sin.

When God answered a prayer of mine in a disappointing way I questioned His fairness and lost confidence that He was caring for me. That lack of confidence translated to an absence of trust — a wrong attitude that robbed me of joy. Blinded by my unexpected sin, I shoved my sinful emotions deep into the pri-

185

vate places of my heart. I couldn't admit I was struggling with trust; I knew that was sin.

We can fool people. But we can't hide sin from God. It's far better to open our hearts and let God search it. He is willing to reveal any sin we're hiding, forgive us, and help us through the pain.

We won't have to look downcast as my son did. We can empty our pockets and look up to God.

Make It Personal

What reasons would you have for hiding secret sin? Is God urging you to expose something? If yes, what is it?

Today I Bring Praise and Thanksgiving For

I Want Those Angels

Read Psalm 91

Key Verse: 91:11 *He will give His angels charge concerning you, to guard you in all your ways.*

I can't recall the movie I was watching on the Inspirational channel. But I vividly remember my reaction.

It was set in Old Testament times. The people were engaged in battle. Chaos ruled. Rapid scene shifts depicted bloodshed and fire. The roar of battle cries, the thunder of galloping warhorses racing into battle, and the screams of the injured echoed through the city.

Then slowly emerging from the smoke and darkness, came two men wearing long red capes. For several seconds, the camera recorded their movement. The battle sounds faded, riveting my attention on the red-caped men. As they studied their surroundings, they moved forward with determination, fully focused on their objective.

Suddenly, the scene shifted to fast motion. The battle sounds grew loud again. And just as fast, both men threw back their red capes, to reveal their suits of armor. Their swords rapidly swung at their targets and killed the enemy soldiers.

The men were angels.

I stood in the privacy of my home and shouted, "Yeah . . . I want those angels!"

For many of us, an angel is a cute little child sitting on a cloud . . . or the shelf of a gift shop. Or maybe it's the handsome adult whose hands play soothing music on a harp.

In life's battles, we don't need a sweet-talking, harp-strumming, angel whispering to our enemy. We want the angel who fights for us.

Depending on the Bible version you use, our key verse contains the words *guard*, *protect*, or *keep*. The *Cambridge English Dictionary* defines *keep* as something we have in our possession.[26] *Keeping* means to repeatedly do something without stopping.

God has charged His angels with the responsibility of keeping, guarding, and protecting continually — without stopping.

Psalm 34:7 says, *The angel of the Lord encamps around those who fear Him, and rescues them.*

We cannot identify with certainty the angels among us, but we can see the evidence of their work. We can also take God at His word. His angels are working on our behalf to kill the schemes of the Evil One.

Make It Personal

Identify your current battle. From what do you need protection?

Today I Bring Praise and Thanksgiving For

Flourish

Read Psalm 92

Key Verse: 92:12 *The righteous man will flourish like the palm tree.*

My friend Jan moved from Florida to western North Carolina. As a passionate photographer, she enjoys taking pictures of her new environment — the beautiful Blue Ridge Mountains.

After living through several rough winters, Jan observed that evergreens and other types of trees snap in half or become uprooted in high winds or a storm. She compared the mountain trees to the trees in Florida. She said, "During tropical storms and hurricanes, palm trees bend over and protect themselves. When the storm is over, they stand back up."

God doesn't use words in careless ways. Every utterance carries meaning. When God says we'll flourish, we can be confident that He will show us how.

At some point, we all experience hurricane-type winds in our life. We may be afraid and secretly wonder if we'll snap in two like the mountain trees. Sometimes our storm resembles heavy mountain snow, pressing against our back. We think we'll be crushed under the heavy weight of our burdens.

God says we'll flourish like the palm tree. Why? Because we bend. We bend our knees in prayer. We bend our independence and self-reliance and humbly ask God to intervene. We bend down in kneeling position and seek protection from God.

Many say that King Solomon was the wisest man to have ever

lived. First Kings 8:54 gives us a glimpse into why he flourished and stood tall among others: *When Solomon had finished praying this entire prayer and supplication to the Lord, he arose from before the altar of the Lord, from kneeling on his knees with his hands spread toward heaven.* His kneeling enabled him to stand.

The storms we face in life are hard, but we don't have to face them alone. When the storm passes, we won't be ripped apart. The sun will shine again, and, like the palm tree, we'll stand back up.

Make It Personal

How will you use this truth in future situations? In what ways will you bend? Will it be for protection or humility?

Today I Bring Praise and Thanksgiving For

Clothed in Majesty

Read Psalm 93

Key Verse: 93:1 *The Lord reigns, He is clothed with majesty.*

The world of fashion is a multi-billion-dollar industry. The clothes we wear help define who we are — our preferred colors, textures, styles. What we put on also identifies who we are for the moment: an athlete, for example, or a professional. Our changing moods can also affect what we decide to put on.

Unlike us, God is unchanging. Our key verse reveals He is always clothed with majesty.

Some characters in books — specifically kings and queens — are called, "Your Majesty." What does *majesty* mean? Majesty is defined as "sovereign power, authority, or dignity." The Bible uses majesty in the context of God. The Hebrew word for majesty, *hoda*, means authority, honor, and splendor.

God wears power, authority, dignity, honor, and splendor. We've witnessed His character through His mighty acts. The Bible also helps us visualize God:

- *I kept looking until thrones were set up, and the Ancient of Days took His seat; His vesture was like white snow and the hair of His head like pure wool. His throne was a blaze with flames, its wheels were a burning fire* (Daniel 7:9).

- *The Lord, high and exalted, seated on a throne; and the train of his robe filled the temple* (Isaiah 6:1).

191

- *In the middle of the lampstands I saw one like a son of man, clothed in a robe reaching to the feet, and girded across His chest with a golden sash. His head and His hair were white like white wool, like snow; and His eyes were like a flame of fire. His feet were like burnished bronze, when it has been made to glow in a furnace, and His voice was like the sound of many waters* (Revelation 1:13–15).

The message for us is that we live under the authority of a powerful God. Regardless of how we're dressed or the mood we're in, we should give God the honor and respect that belongs to Him alone.

Make It Personal

How does today's reading change or enhance your view of God?

Today I Bring Praise and Thanksgiving For

God Sees You

Read Psalm 94

Key Verses: 94:7–9 *They have said, "The Lord does not see, nor does the God of Jacob pay heed." Pay heed, you senseless among the people; and when will you understand, stupid ones? He who planted the ear, does He not hear? He who formed the eye, does He not see?*

Hagar was pregnant and alone — at least, emotionally. Although one of Abram's wives, she wasn't as favored as Sarai, who emotionally abused her, possibly because of jealousy. Hagar returned fire by flaunting her pregnancy. Distraught and weary, and with few resources, she fled to the desert and called on God. He heard her cries and answered: *You will bear a son; and you shall call his name Ishmael, because the Lord has given heed to your affliction* (Genesis 16:11). Hagar responded with a spot-on observation: *"You are a God who sees"* (Genesis 16:13).

Stupidity says God doesn't see. God's Word says He does.

Many of us can relate to being in a "desert" season. We crave an escape from our present affliction. Although surrounded by dozens of people, we feel alone, helpless, and desperate. Does God see?

He sees. He knows the number of hairs on our head and every tear we shed. He sees our pain and our exclusion. He knows our isolation, loss, and emptiness. He sees it all.

Before becoming Abram's second wife, Hagar had been a slave and in a position of weakness. In her current situation, she revisited her weakness — defenseless and without hope. Yet God saw Hagar in the desert, and His faithfulness to her was like a stream of water in a dry place. Sixteen years later and again in a hopeless state, Hagar and her son were forced to return to the desert. With impending death at the forefront of her mind, she called out to God. Again, God heard her cries. While Hagar and her son lay dying of thirst, God opened her eyes to see a nearby well (Genesis 21:15–21).

May God open our eyes, allowing us to draw from the well that sustains us in our dry places. We may desire to escape our situation but we can never escape God's gaze. He sees us. He sees you.

Make It Personal

Do you believe God sees what you're going through? Why or why not? In what ways has God refreshed you?

Today I Bring Praise and Thanksgiving For

The Twisted, Rocky Path

Read Psalm 95

Key Verse: 95:8 *Do not harden your hearts.*

*D*o you need a new start or a different direction?

The Israelites received many new starts. They were finally free from bondage to the Egyptians, when their leader, Moses, led them to the desert. From there, they had an eleven-day journey into Canaan, the Promised Land. But they rebelled against Moses and God, despite having witnessed miracles that provided their freedom and enabled them to survive. They crossed through the middle of a sea, ate bread that descended from heaven, and drank water gushing from a rock. Still, unbelief, doubt, and selfish desires captured their hearts. In fact, their hearts were hard toward God.

The consequence was severe. The Israelites remained in the wilderness forty years. After this time, God kept His word and allowed them to enter the Promised Land. Although they chose the long, hard, twisted path, God still moved them from point A to point B.

Have you been wandering in the wilderness for a long time? Poor choices squander time, opportunities, and blessings. But God still moves us from point A to point B — His perfect, promised plan. Hebrews 3:7–9 tells us, *Therefore, just as the Holy Spirit says, "Today if you hear His voice, do not harden your hearts as when they provoked Me, as in the day of trial in the wilderness, where your fathers tried Me by testing Me, and saw my works for forty years.*

The writer of Hebrews warns us not to follow the example of unfaithful Israel and harden our hearts. Disobedience kept them from God's intended blessings for years. Even if rocks in our path have hurt our feet, God will bandage our wounds.

Proverbs 4:11–13 tells us, *I will teach you wisdom's ways and lead you in straight paths. When you walk, you won't be held back; when you run, you won't stumble. Take hold of my instructions; don't let them go. Guard them, for they are the key to life* (NLT).

It's never too late to trust God to straighten the path and arrive at point B!

Make It Personal

Back to the initital question: Are you ready for a new start? If yes, what's your strategy?

Today I Bring Praise and Thanksgiving For

Sing of God's Faithfulness

Read Psalm 96

Key Verse: 96:1 *Sing to the Lord a new song.*

*W*ith each season — good or bad — we have the opportunity to reflect on God's faithful work in our lives. The psalmist encourages us to sing of His faithfulness.

How has God recently been faithful to you? What new thing has He done? As God shows Himself faithful, it justifies a new song.

As we age, we gain life experiences. With each experience we're able to see God's faithful work in our lives. We may see His character in ways we'd never realized. And soon we have a reservoir of God's goodness from which we can pull fantastic memories. We read about God's faithfulness and miraculous deeds in Bible stories. One example is Hannah. She prayed for a son and God was faithful and gave her Samuel. Her song of praise is recorded in 1 Samuel 2:1: *My heart rejoices in the Lord; in the Lord my horn is lifted high. My mouth boasts over my enemies, for I delight in your deliverance* (NIV). Bible stories teach us about God's faithfulness, but it's a whole new level of understanding when we personally experience His activity.

To which of these can you relate?

- God faithfully remained by your side when your life was falling apart.

- God extended mercy when He intervened and protected you from injustice.
- God answered your prayer.
- God stood with you when others abandoned you.
- God saved you from a mistake by not granting your request.

We sing new songs of praise when we're ending a season of pain and suffering.

We sing new songs of praise with each answered prayer.

We sing new songs of praise when miracles happen.

We sing new songs of praise when we desperately need Him.

And yet, this is only the beginning. As long as we live on this earth, God will continue to be faithful. And His faithfulness will compel us to sing new songs of praise. Let's celebrate with this popular hymn, "Great Is Thy Faithfulness."

Make It Personal

What is your favorite worship or praise song?

Today I Bring Praise and Thanksgiving For

Unsuspected Idols

Read Psalm 97

Key Verse: 97:7 *Let all those be ashamed who serve graven images, who boast themselves of idols.*

Some people proudly decorate their shelves, tables, and yards with statues they claim are gods. The people who make them create the eyes; they carve out ears; they sculpt the lips; they meticulously fashion the nose. But both the idols and the creators who make them are completely powerless — for power comes from the One True God. Psalm 115 also mentions these idols: *They have mouths, but cannot speak, eyes, but cannot see. They have ears, but cannot hear, noses, but cannot smell* (vv. 5–6 NIV).

We may pity those who put their faith in a powerless, emotionless, and deaf god. But do we place our hope in idols too? Are there not-so-obvious idols tucked within our hearts, hidden from onlookers and definitely not on display? No one knows they exist — maybe even ourselves.

An idol is anything we make more important than God — power, money, authority, recognition, a person, a possession, or even our ego. Whatever we serve or make sacrifices for is our idol. When we depend on the power of something or someone other than God, that thing or person becomes an idol.

In the context of Exodus 32, the Israelites made golden idols and worshipped them instead of God. God is jealous for what already belongs to Him — His people and their worship (Exodus 34:14). He won't share His glory with another.

Idols can't last.

Thankfully, we can ask God to reveal to us anything that has inadvertently become more important than Him and empower us to remove this idol from our lives.

Make It Personal

What are some practical ways to keep your devotion to God in proper order?

Today I Bring Praise and Thanksgiving For

Righteous Judgment

Read Psalm 98

Key Verse: 98:9 *He is coming to judge the earth; He will judge the world with righteousness.*

The bad news first — we all deserve judgment and death. The Bible tells us in Romans 3:10, *There is none righteous, not even one.* Born with a sinful nature, we deserve separation from a perfect God.

Now, the good news. God made a way for us to spend eternity with Him. Ephesians 2:4–5 tells us, *God, being rich in mercy, because of His great love with which He loved us, even when we were dead in our transgressions, made us alive together with Christ (by grace you have been saved).*

Second Peter 3:9 tells us: *The Lord . . . is patient toward you . . . not wishing any to perish but for all to come to repentance.*

God didn't give us the death we deserve. In His mercy, God sent His Son Jesus as the sacrifice and punishment for our sin. Salvation is a free gift (Romans 6:23). This is grace — getting what we don't deserve. That was His part. Our part is to accept God's gift — a gift that is free to us but wasn't cheap for Jesus, who gave His life so we could have everlasting life.

We don't need to fear God's judgment. We can do as the psalmist did — shout victory and sing because God is a righteous judge. We can accept what He has to offer.

- First, we admit we're sinners and confess our sins. First John 1:9 tells us that *if we confess our sins, He is faithful*

*and righteous to forgive us our sins and to cleanse us from all
unrighteousness.*

- Next, we accept the truth about Jesus. First Corinthians
  15:4 tells us *that He was buried, and that He was raised on
  the third day according to the Scriptures.*

- Third, we choose to receive God's gift of salvation.
  Romans 10:9 says *if you confess with your mouth Je-
  sus as* Lord, and believe in your heart that God raised
  Him from the dead, you will be saved.

- Then, we follow Jesus by reading His Word and living a
  life of obedience to Him.

This decision to accept God's free gift is the best decision of
your life.

Make It Personal

Do you believe that Jesus died for you so that you could
be with Him forever? If not, what is preventing you from
making this decision?

Today I Bring Praise and Thanksgiving For

Invitation to Worship

Read Psalm 99

Key Verse: 99:9 *Exalt the Lord our God and worship at His holy mountain, for the Lord our God is holy.*

One of my favorite parts of the movie *Esther* is when King Ahasuerus (also named Xerses) extends his scepter to Queen Esther, inviting her to approach the throne. Although she was his wife, it was forbidden for her to enter the king's throne room without permission. Esther boldly took the risk. She knew that if Ahasuerus denied her, she'd be put to death. That was the law in his empire.

Similarly, no person could approach God, whose glory and presence dwelt in the temple on Mount Zion. His presence was concealed by a large veil, or temple curtain that separated the Holy of Holies from the rest of the temple. Only once a year, on the Day of Atonement, was the high priest allowed to go beyond the veil to make a sacrifice for the people. The priests worshipped closest to the bronze altar. Then there was an area for the Jews. Outside was a place designated for the common worshippers.

Today we no longer worship in this way. God permanently extended His scepter when Jesus was crucified. At His death, the Holy of Holies' curtain was torn from top to the bottom, giving people direct access to God. Through Jesus, we no longer need a priest to go before us, for Jesus is our high priest. And we no longer wait outside the sanctuary away from God's presence. Instead, God invites us to approach His throne — for prayer, help, and worship (Hebrews 4:16).

How amazing. We have an open invitation to boldly enter the throne room of God — without fear or penalty. For believers this is a throne of grace.

Have we taken our freedom to worship for granted? Have we neglected to accept God's extended scepter by withholding the adoration and reverence that is due Him? God is holy, totally set apart. Yet He chooses to dwell with His people. What an extraordinary privilege to come before God.

Make It Personal

How can you respond to God's invitation to approach Him?

Today I Bring Praise and Thanksgiving For

Is God Still Good?

Read Psalm 100

Key Verse: 100:5 *The Lord is good; His lovingkindness is everlasting and His faithfulness to all generations.*

At 4:00 A.M. the sound of the ringing phone jolted my husband and me from a sound sleep. My son, driving to his job early in the morning, had been involved in a storm-related accident. Three enormous trees had been uprooted and hurled onto his path. Without time to brake, he crashed into them, which propelled his vehicle into the air. His truck landed on the passenger side, then skidded thirty feet. Although the glass in the windows was shattered, he emerged from the wreckage without a scratch. God spared my son's life. In times like these we agree that God is good.

But what about when the outcome is bad. Is God still good? My friend Eleanor shares her story:

> The officers arrived at my home at 2:00 A.M. with the horrifying news that my twenty-eight-year-old son had been in an accident near our house and hadn't survived. A swarm of emotions, including anger, enveloped me for a couple of years. At first, I tried to hide from the pain. But then I turned to God. Today, God continues to pour out His compassion so that I am filled with peace and joy. God has never failed to show up. I am reminded that I will see Justin again. On the days I can't catch my breath and am overwhelmed with the memory, God

meets me in the most tender of ways. God has cared for me as a father would his daughter. Daily, I experience His goodness. As a result, I am stronger than I have ever been.

No matter what happens, always lean on him. I can't think of anything worse than the sudden death of a child. It has changed me forever and I could not even take my next breath without Jesus. Trust Him with the big things and trust Him with the small things, I promise He will hold you up.

Ephesians 2:4 became alive for Eleanor. God's love and mercy touched her. And she believed Psalm 119:68 which tells us, *You are good, and what You do is good.*

In our humanity, it's difficult to comprehend His goodness. All we can do is choose to believe that God is good. Even if we don't understand God's ways, it doesn't mean He isn't who He says He is. Through the blur of tears and suffering, He will show us His goodness.

Make It Personal

When is it difficult to believe that God is good? When is it easy? Ask Him to help you believe.

Today I Bring Praise and Thanksgiving For

I Will

Read Psalm 101

Key Verse: 101:3 *I will set no worthless thing before my eyes.*

*F*rom the time my children were young, I wrote Bible verses on index cards and placed them by each of our plates at dinner. Sometimes I selected the verses because their content was worthy of memorizing. But other times, I intentionally chose a verse to meet a particular need or help with a crucial decision.

One verse I used quite often was Psalm 101:3: *I will set no worthless thing before my eyes.*

When any of my children wanted to go to a movie with friends, I selected this verse. After we discussed it, they helped make the decision about attending. Participating in the decision process made them feel empowered and respected.

One night I passed this verse on to my youngest child and asked him to read the reviews about a movie he wanted to see, which contained foul language. After reading the reviews he said, "What a waste of money to sit there with my fingers in my ears the whole time!"

Nine times in this psalm, David said, "I will." That indicated his desire to be faithfully committed. But his behavior didn't always reflect his desire, and sometimes he failed to live righteously.

We have the same problem. We strive to focus on worthy aspirations, yet we become distracted by worthless desires.

With God's help, our priorities, the people we admire, and how we use our time, will be worthy of our attention.

Philippians 4:8 tells us, *Whatever is true, whatever is honorable, whatever is right, whatever is pure, whatever is lovely, whatever is of good repute, if there is any excellence and if anything worthy of praise, dwell on these things.*

Make It Personal

What worthwhile activities do you participate? What, if anything, is worthless?

Today I Bring Praise and Thanksgiving For

Not So Alone in My Loneliness

Read Psalm 102

Key Verse: 102:7 *I lie awake, I have become like a lonely bird on a housetop.*

*L*oneliness can subtly creep in like fog descending on a mountain early in the morning. A CBS news segment reported that seventy-two percent of Americans feel lonely.[27] Loneliness, however, isn't exclusive to one group of people — it occurs in every culture.

Loneliness can be defined as "sadness from being alone." But loneliness is also a state of mind. Craving something we need or adjusting to an unmet expectation can leave us feeling abandoned and isolated. We can be lonely even though we're surrounded by people.

We're wired for connection. Technology may appear to instantly connect people, but behind the screen, social media can make us feel more disconnected. Secular articles offer suggestions for dealing with loneliness. One psychology magazine said that it helps to meditate and serve others.[28] Weren't those God's ideas?

God's idea is to fill our empty and lonely hearts by:

- Talking to God. First Peter 5:7 tells us, *Cast all your anxiety on him, because He cares for you* (NIV). Turning to

God with any problem is the right thing to do. Proverbs 14:10 tells us, *The heart knows its own bitterness, and a stranger does not share its joy*. God is not a stranger. He created each of us uniquely and He knows exactly how we feel. He desires a relationship with us, and this intimacy happens every time we go to Him — with any problem we have.

- Serving others. Galatians 5:13 tells us, *Through love serve one another*. Studies show that by serving others, we find satisfaction, purpose and identity. One study followed people who volunteered for five years, and reported these people as feeling "happy."

- Putting our hope in God. First Timothy 5:5 uses an example of a widow who has lost support of family. Feeling alone, she set her hope in God.

If we're feeling like the lonely bird the psalmist mentioned, we can ask God to fill our emptiness and show us specifically what to do.

Make It Personal

Reflect on a time you felt lonely. Were you physically alone or surrounded by people? Can you identify the source of your loneliness? If yes, what was it? If no, ask God to direct you.

Today I Bring Praise and Thanksgiving For

God Remembers We're Dust

Read Psalm 103

Key Verse: 103:14 *For He knows our frame; He is mindful that we are dust.*

When we think of dust, we might think about the dust in our home — particles of skin, dust mites.

When God uses dust, however, it carries deeper meaning. We first read about dust in Genesis 2:7: *Then the Lord God formed man of dust from the ground, and breathed into his nostrils the breath of life; and man became a living being.*

The Hebrew word for dust, *aphar*, means "dry earth, dirt; clay, mud, ashes, dust, ground, powder, rubbish." Dust, then, is substance broken down to its lowest form.

From a seemingly insignificant word, we see astonishing implications:

- Apart from God, we're frail and weak. Compared to God, we're the lowest. If He were to let go of us, we'd be destroyed. We need His help, but God doesn't hold that against us.

- God doesn't expect us to live independent of Him. He knows how little we can do apart from Him. We're easily broken down.

- Since we're dust, God shows His compassion. Psalm 103:10 tells us, *He has not dealt with us according to our sins, nor rewarded us according to our iniquities.* He doesn't deal with us according to our sins because the *Son was pierced through for our transgressions, He was crushed for our iniquities; The chastening for our well-being fell* upon Him, *and by His scourging we are healed* . . . *But the Lord has caused the iniquity of us all to fall on Him* (Isaiah 53:5–6).

- Dust mixed with water makes clay. Clay is a moldable substance. Isaiah 64:8 tells us, *You are our Father, we are the clay, and You our potter; and all of us are the work of Your hand.* God is the potter and we're His clay. In another instance, God said to Jeremiah, *"Arise and go down to the potter's house, and there I will announce My words to you."* Jeremiah said, *Then I went down to the potter's house, and there he was, making something on the wheel. But the vessel that he was making of clay was spoiled in the hand of the potter; so he remade it into another vessel, as it pleased the potter to make* (Jeremiah 18:1–4). God said He remolds us; He continues to shape us until we're a vessel that pleases Him.

We were made from dust. And what a tremendous blessing to know God remembers!

Make It Personal

Which of the four dust implications listed best describes what you need to remember today?

Today I Bring Praise and Thanksgiving For

Bless God

Read Psalm 104

Key Verse: 104:1 *Bless the Lord, O my soul! O Lord, my God, You are very great.*

I'm so blessed is an expression we hear when people talk about anything good. But we hear of the following blessings less frequently.

- God forgives and takes away our guilt and shame.
- God heals and redeems our life.
- God is kind and compassionate.
- God shows mercy by not giving us what we deserve.
- God is slow to anger.

But our key verse directs us to bless God. How can we who have nothing bless God who has everything?

Wiersbe answered this question: "'To bless the Lord' means to delight His heart by expressing gratitude for all He is and all He does."

We're encouraged when others thank us for the gifts we give and the necessities we provide. We love it when others notice our help with a project or fixing a meal.

Our heavenly Father has done more for us than we could ever do for others. And telling Him so is how we bless Him.

John Piper wrote: "My thesis is that in the Scripture when God 'blesses' men they are thereby helped and strengthened and made better off than they were before, but when men 'bless' God He is not helped or strengthened or made better off. Rather, man's blessing God is an 'expression of praising thankfulness.' It is an 'exclamation of gratitude and admiration.'"

Our perfect Father blesses us. But isn't it wonderful that He doesn't expect perfection in return? When we bring our praise and thanks to Him, that's blessing enough.

Then we can say, *Blessed be the God and Father of our Lord Jesus Christ, the Father of mercies and God of all comfort* (2 Corinthians 1:3).

Make It Personal

How can you bless God today? What can you thank Him for that will delight His heart?

Today I Bring Praise and Thanksgiving For

Being Found

Read Psalm 105

Key Verse: 105:4 *Seek the Lord and His strength; seek His face continually.*

I loved playing "Hide and Seek" when I was a child. We didn't travel far to hide — mostly we hid in the backyard. The swing set and trees easily concealed our whereabouts. The rules were simple. We needed two or more players. While the others hid, one person covered his or her eyes, counted to ten then tried to find everyone else.

When my friends and I played, we tried to hide so we weren't easily found. But God doesn't hide so that we can't find Him. He wants us to find Him when we seek Him. He longs to be found so He can reveal His character. He wants us to discern His voice so we can hear instruction, obey it, and be blessed. In Jeremiah 29:13 we read, *You will seek Me and find Me when you search for Me with all your heart.*

Are we seeking God? Finding Him may be difficult in an environment filled with many distractions. People with differing viewpoints about who God is can cast confusion if they're the ones to whom we listen. Busying ourselves with activities leaves no room for God. Hiding our feelings from Him denies us the opportunity to change or grow.

We can begin seeking God by prioritizing. Matthew 6:33 tells us, *Seek first His kingdom and His righteousness, and all these things will be added to you.*

Seek God and ask Him to reveal Himself. Cut down on busy-ness, which makes it difficult to find time to have a relationship with God.

We might think that we need to clean up our act or change our behavior before we search for God. But God gives us a clean start. All we have to do is come to Him. Psalm 14:2 says *the Lord has looked down from heaven upon the sons of men to see if there are any who understand, who seek after God.*

When we seek God, we'll find Him. And in this "Hide and Seek" activity, we'll always come out a winner.

Make It Personal

Are you seeking a more intimate relationship with God? What steps will you take to find Him?

Today I Bring Praise and Thanksgiving For

Spiritual Amnesia

Read Psalm 106

Key Verse: 106:21 *They forgot their Savior.*

They whined and cried, grumbled and complained. Not preschool children — the Israelites — approximately two million Jewish people whom God had freed from captivity. We've read about these miraculous works before. Let's recap: God sent plagues to ensure their freedom. After their deliverance, God stayed with them on their journey. He led them with a cloud by day and a pillar of fire by night. He opened the Red Sea so they could cross safely to the other side. In the desert, He split the rocks and water gushed out. God fed them with manna and meat that rained down from the sky. He took care of their clothes and their feet. The Israelites witnessed God's provision, compassion, miraculous signs and wonders, yet they continued to sin. More of their shocking response is recorded in verses 24-25: *Then they despised the pleasant land; they did not believe in His word, but grumbled in their tents; they did not listen to the voice of the Lord .*

Go back several chapters to Psalm 78 and you'll read that they even mocked God (verse 19).

For any group of people to experience God's miraculous provision and then be so ungrateful is unfathomable. More like illogical . . . bizarre.

Could we resemble those grumbling Israelites? Do we suffer from spiritual amnesia? Do we forget what God has done for us in the past and complain about our current circumstances? We don't literally forget — it's more like we fail to be awed or amazed by the manner in which God made a path for us when there appeared to be no way, or the method in which He turned something bad into something good and useful.

Thankfully, God remembers that we were made from dust (Psalm 103:14) and in our humanness, we are prone to forget. But He doesn't hold our forgetfulness against us. In His mercy and compassion, God acts on our behalf again and again.

Let's remember and reflect on the goodness of God. Let's recall that God was faithful in the past, and He will be faithful now and in the future. Then praise will replace complaints and reflection will restore hope.

Make It Personal

Has complaining become a regular habit? What has happened in your past that still makes you thankful? How does this reflection bring you hope?

Today I Bring Praise and Thanksgiving For

Unfailing Love

Read Psalm 107

Key Verse: 107:1 *Oh give thanks to the Lord, for He is good, for His lovingkindness is everlasting.*

No matter how we think others see us, God sees us through eyes of love. In this psalm alone, God's unfailing love is mentioned five times.

Most would agree that God loves the world — this vast, huge world. However, choosing to believe that God loves us personally may be difficult. The fact that God uniquely designed each of us with a purpose may be hard to grasp.

Because we live in a fallen world, bad things happen. Adversity might prompt us to feel forgotten or unloved by God. But feelings can deceive us. Satan can use our negative thoughts to convince us that we're not worthy of God's love.

But God's Word tells us otherwise. It affirms His love:

- *God demonstrates His own love toward us, in that while we were yet sinners, Christ died for us.* (Romans 5:8)

- *We are His workmanship.* (Ephesians 2:10)

- *I have loved you with an everlasting love.* (Jeremiah 31:3)

- *The Lord your God turned the curse into a blessing for you because the Lord your God loves you.* (Deuteronomy 23:5)

When Satan tells us that we don't matter, remember that God's Word says we do. When the world says we don't measure up, God says we do. The next time we feel insignificant or unworthy, we can recall that we're God's masterpiece, and He paid a great price for us. When the world says we'll never fit in, God says that as His child, we fit in perfectly. God knows us better than anyone else, including ourselves, and He still loves us. His love can't fail. Choose to believe it.

Make It Personal

How would your life look different if you applied the truths listed above?

Today I Bring Praise and Thanksgiving For

Steadfast

Read Psalm 108

Key Verse: 108:1 *My heart is steadfast, O God.*

With a heavy schedule, a barrage of problems, and never-ending responsibilities, deciphering which goals and plans to prioritize can be difficult. In some cases, we hesitate to begin a new endeavor, passion, or calling God placed on our hearts. We're fearful to run with something new, but equally afraid not to. Disillusioned with or exhausted by our current priorities, we might even abandon what God called us to actively engage in:

- praying for a prodigal
- finishing a project
- leading a ministry
- becoming financially stable
- working on a relationship
- believing we're making a difference
- continuing to have hope

But God calls us to be steadfast. Steadfastness isn't a word we use every day, and when we do, it's usually in the context of God's character. Steadfast is defined as "immoveable and unchanging." Synonyms include loyal, faithful, devoted, dependable, and trustworthy — a perfect description of God.

Steadfastness is similar in definition to perseverance. The Hebrew word is *emunah*, meaning steady, firm, and faithful.

David declared that his heart was steadfast toward God. Is our devotion to God as loyal? Do we seek His direction first and persevere? For our heart to be loyal and steadfast to God means we remain steady and grounded in our faith even when it's not popular or it doesn't make sense. It means we persevere with an unwavering commitment to finish what God called us to do.

For strength to be steadfast, we'll need to stay close to God by reading His Word, praying about what His Word means, and actively applying His Word to our life — especially when times are hard.

Like David, let's strive to be steadfast in our thinking and live with wholehearted devotion.

Make It Personal

In what area do you need to be steadfast?

Today I Bring Praise and Thanksgiving For

I'm In Prayer

Read Psalm 109

Key Verse: 109:4 *But I am in prayer.*

How often do we turn off technology and find quiet time free from distractions to pray? Life is busy and full of demanding activities. We might quickly pray while heading out to numerous other responsibilities or while multi-tasking. There's nothing wrong with quick prayers or praying while doing other things. But focused prayer often takes a back seat to other priorities. It may even become the last thing we do.

We need to make time for concentrated prayer — prayer without distractions — because prayer is powerful.

- Prayer can make possible the seemingly impossible. Joni Eareckson Tada, a quadriplegic, author, and founder of Joni and Friends, puts it like this: "I don't move a muscle while I'm in bed, but I help move the hand of God here and abroad [with my prayers]."[29] Prayer releases us from manipulation, or control, or trying to do things ourselves. Prayer alone will move the hand of God.

- Prayer changes people and outcomes. Our prayers for others may be the only prayers they get. If we thought we could change another person's life by genuine prayer, we would. Choose to believe that prayer makes a difference. When we communicate with God, He opens our eyes to see in ways we hadn't seen before, and this changes us.

- Prayer strengthens our relationship with God. He knows what we need. But He wants us to ask Him to meet our needs so He can be in relationship with us.

- Sometimes we're unable to articulate what is in our hearts. Perhaps we don't know the words to use. In times like these, the Holy Spirit intercedes for us.

- Prayer invites God to intervene. God won't take control of what we won't give to Him. When we pray, we humbly submit to God's strong, holy authority.

Corrie Ten Boom, who saved the lives of an estimated 800 Jews during World War II, understood the power of prayer. She wrote, "If the devil cannot make us bad, he will make us busy. *Don't pray [only] when you feel like it. Have an appointment with the Lord and keep it. A man is powerful on his knees.*"[30]

Make the appointment. Be mighty in strength today.

Make It Personal

What keeps you from spending time in prayer?

Today I Bring Praise and Thanksgiving For

Our Unchanging God

Read Psalm 110

Key Verse: 110:4 *The Lord has sworn and will not change His mind.*

We live in an ever-changing world. The changing seasons bring outstanding beauty and fresh opportunity. Technology changes the way we communicate, what we see, and how doctors treat our illnesses. Fashion trends and hairstyles evolve. Our health changes. Our skin reveals the decades with wrinkles and age spots. Family meals change based on who shows up to eat. Our personal desires, plans, long-and-short-term goals must be modified. Change is inevitable. No one is unaffected.

Except God.

From the beginning of time as we know it, God has remained unchanged — a constant being. Completely consistent.

His love for us is steadfast. His pursuit of us hasn't changed. His mercy flows without end. His promises haven't been retracted. His grace continues.

- *I, the Lord, do not change; therefore you, O sons of Jacob, are not consumed.* (Malachi 3:6)

- *Jesus Christ is the same yesterday and today and forever.* (Hebrews 13:8)

- *God is not a man, that He should lie, nor a son of man, that He should repent; has He said, and will He not do it? Or has He spoken, and will He not make it good?* (Numbers 23:19)

225

- *You founded the earth, and the heavens are the work of Your hands. Even they will perish, but You endure; and all of them will wear out like a garment; like clothing You will change them and they will be changed. But You are the same, and Your years will not come to an end .*(Psalm 102:25–27)

God doesn't have to change His ways or His mind because He doesn't make mistakes. What He spoke to men and women in the Bible, He speaks to us today.

Believe it. Don't give up or lose hope. God hasn't changed His mind about our worth, or our purpose. He's not fed up with our ever-changing moods and desires. God stays true to His character and His standards.

Make It Personal

Do you feel like God has changed His mind about you? If so, where do you think this comes from?

Today I Bring Praise and Thanksgiving For

Wisdom

Read Psalm 111

Key Verse: 111:10 *The fear of the Lord is the beginning of wisdom; a good understanding have all those who do His commandments; His praise endures forever.*

*I*n many cultures the owl represents wisdom. But there is a deeper meaning to the symbolism of the owl. One Christian tradition says that owls represent the wisdom of Christ.

God gives *all of us* wisdom (James 1:5). Could you use wisdom in any of these areas?

- Relationships
- Choosing your words
- Work decisions
- Discovering your purpose
- Medical treatment
- Sharing the gospel
- Handling conflict

We need to know what to do and how to live. But people who have acquired knowledge aren't always wise. Free Dictionary. com defines knowledge as, "information gained through experience, reasoning, or acquaintance" and wisdom as "the ability to discern or judge what is true, right, or lasting."[31]

Wiersbe explains these differences this way: "Knowledge enables us to take things apart, but wisdom enables us to put things together and relate truth to daily life."[32] Additionally, author and preacher Vance Havner says, "If you lack knowledge, go to school. If you lack wisdom, get on your knees! Knowledge is not wisdom. Wisdom is the proper use of knowledge."[33]

Wisdom, then, is knowing and applying truth and may have nothing to do with chronological age. Age and maturity aren't synonymous with wisdom.

In this way, a younger Christian woman can be spiritually wiser than her elder. Any woman who chooses to leave God out of her daily life, remains unchanged — and unwise. Birthdays don't make us wise; a relationship with Jesus does.

Spending time with God each day and learning to fear — respect and reverence — Him is the way to become spiritually wise. And wisdom leads to obedience, which results in blessings.

Seeking wisdom from God will make us look different too. Ecclesiastes 8:1 tells us, *Wisdom illumines him and causes his stern face to beam.*

Make It Personal

What are you seeking wisdom for today? To whom will you turn to get it?

Today I Bring Praise and Thanksgiving For

When Things Don't Make Sense

Read Psalm 112

Key Verses: 112:6–7 *He will never be shaken; the righteous will be remembered forever. He will not fear evil tidings; his heart is steadfast, trusting in the Lord.*

Once my husband asked our teenage son, Will, to call the dog in for the night. Will whistled first, then yelled, "Buddy, Buddy, come on, Buddy." It was a dark, moonless night, but Will saw Buddy's dark figure pacing back and forth at the edge of the dim glow cast by the garage light. Buddy was barking loudly, and Will couldn't understand why he wouldn't come in.

Suspecting something was wrong, Will called his dad and said, "This doesn't make sense. Buddy just keeps pacing back and forth in front of the garage."

After he got a good look, my husband's expression turned from curious to shocked. Then he said, "That's not Buddy — that's a bear!"

Although Will was momentarily shaken, the bear finally ran away.

Often our lives are shaken when circumstances don't make sense. Despite being obedient to the Lord, we have unexpected hardship. We seek God's will but there's still uncertainty. Or perhaps we're looking at a situation through dirty lenses and can't see clearly. We want to be strong, but we pace the floor with fear. As we call out to God, our rapidly beating heart is all we feel.

Isaiah 26:3 tells us, *The steadfast of mind You will keep in perfect peace, because he trusts in You.*

Take hold of peace and trust God when it's difficult to see in the dark. This is faith — to trust God and accept that His thoughts and ways are different from ours (Isaiah 55:8). We don't have to understand, but we can trust Him when He says He'll never make a mistake or leave us alone, especially when things don't make sense.

Make It Personal

In what ways do you have a bear-of-a-problem? What is bringing confusion? What is hard to see in the darkness?

Today I Bring Praise and Thanksgiving For

Rejected

Read Psalm 113

Key Verse: 113:7 *He raises the poor from the dust and lifts the needy from the ash heap.*

*M*ost of us can remember a time of rejection. Some of us recover, but for many, the emotional scars keep us from feeling wanted, accepted, or worthy.

Whether intentional or not, when we refuse to acknowledge someone, we are, in fact, rejecting that person. Rejection occurs when:

- We're not invited to lunch with the rest of our co-workers.
- Our ideas aren't heard.
- There's no one to sit with in church.
- We don't make the team.
- The job was offered to someone else.
- A spouse leaves.

Even when others inadvertently decline to make eye contact or say *hello* in passing, we can feel as if they think we're not worth their time.

In Bible times, sprinkling ashes on one's head or sitting in a pile of ashes symbolized grief, rejection, humiliation, or repentance. In the Bible, wearing ashes is similar to our wearing black to a funeral — it signifies on the outside what we're feeling on the inside.

Wiersbe describes the ash heap mentioned in our key verse as "the gathering place of the outcasts . . . the one place that people avoided going near."[34] To be there would mean we've been rejected.

But God. God stoops and lifts us out of the ash heap of rejection and brokenness. Yes, praise the Lord, for He lifts up the poor in spirit.

The prophecy about the coming Messiah in Isaiah 53:3 tells us, *He was despised and forsaken of men, a man of sorrows and acquainted with grief; and like one from whom men hide their face He was despised, and we did not esteem Him.* Jesus was rejected so He can relate to us. He took rejection so we wouldn't have to.

We can't let others' opinions determine our worth. We must choose to focus on how God has accepted us and made us beautiful.

Make It Personal

What does it mean to you that God stoops and lifts us from the ashes?

Today I Bring Praise and Thanksgiving For

God Goes Before Us

Read Psalm 114

Key Verses: 114:7–8 *Tremble O earth, before the Lord, before the God of Jacob, who turned the rock into a pool of water, the flint into a fountain of water.*

One of the most important concepts we can learn about God is that He goes before us.

Many years ago, God went before me and solved a problem, before I knew a problem existed. Interpreting for college students paid for all but the last semester of my college education, so I was forced to secure a college loan, even though paying it back would be difficult. Little did I know that for five years, God would strategically position me in a job that would cause my college loan to be forgiven because of the conditions of that job. God answered my prayer for financial provision even before I asked. This is who God is. He went before me.

Before the Israelites were freed, God went before them and prepared their way. He met them at the Red Sea, the Jordan River, the mountains, and the desert — all hopeless places. God had miracles ready to meet their needs. Who else can make water gush from a rock?

What mountain is in your way? What body of water are you trying to cross? The same God who led Moses, also leads us. God says, *I will go before you and make the rough places smooth; I will shatter the doors of bronze and cut through their iron bars* (Isaiah 45:2).

God goes before us — into the courtroom, job interview,

doctor's office, school, and every other place we go. No matter how impossible our situation, God moves mountains and parts seas that obstruct our path to His will. Isaiah 40:3 tells us, *Clear the way for the Lord in the wilderness; make smooth in the desert a highway for our God.* Imagine . . . a highway!

Before I knew my problem existed, God answered it. Before the Israelites got to the desert, God cleared their path. Isaiah 65:24 tells us, *I will answer them before they even call to me. While they are still talking about their needs, I will go ahead and answer their prayers* (NLT)!

Whatever you are heading into, God is already there — and He's made a way to get through.

Make It Personal

Do you believe God goes before you? Why or why not? What miracle are you seeking?

Today I Bring Praise and Thanksgiving For

Mindful

Read Psalm 115

Key Verse: 115:12 *The Lord has been mindful of us.*

*H*ave you ever been deep in thought while doing a task that you wondered how the task got done? The chore was mindless and routine and you were on automatic pilot while doing it.

But God is never on automatic pilot and His tasks are never routine or without thought. He is intentional and at all times wholly mindful of us.

Mindful is defined as "the practice of maintaining a non-judgmental state of heightened or complete awareness of one's thoughts, emotions, or experiences on a moment-to-moment basis; a state of awareness." In the Hebrew, mindful means to remember. In this context, mindful means we're always on God's heart. His faithfulness proves He remembers us.

Psalm 8:4 asks, *What is mankind that you are mindful of them, human beings that you care for them?* (NIV) When the psalmist asks, "What is man that you are mindful," he's comparing mankind's frailty with the greatness of God. It doesn't make sense to have a holy God think about us the way He does, but He tells us in Isaiah 49:16, *I have inscribed you on the palms of My hands.*

Do we understand the significance of the psalmist's question or God's inscription on His hand? He is aware of our thoughts, emotions, and actions on a continuous basis. He is mindful, even when we're not mindful of Him. That, in and of itself,

235

is a miracle—that in spite of the times we disregard His commands, neglect or ignore His leading, He remains mindful. He watches us; we're on His radar; He knows every detail of our lives and He is thinking about them! *Even the very hairs of your head are all numbered* (Matthew 10:30).

Don't leave this thought—allow it to grip your mind and captivate your heart. As His most prized possession, He is always mindful of us.

Make It Personal

Do you feel like God is unaware of you? Why or why not?

Today I Bring Praise and Thanksgiving For

He Inclines His Ear

Read Psalm 116

Key Verses: 116:1–2 *I love the Lord, because He hears my voice and my supplications. Because He has inclined His ear to me, therefore I shall call upon Him as long as I live.*

Children say what they think. In many ways, they are good examples of speaking truth from a pure heart. And sometimes they do what we wish we could do when we feel someone isn't listening: they take our face in their hands and move it toward them. Instant eye contact. Body language that speaks: *Listen to me!*

God isn't like the busy adult whose children have to fight for attention. The Bible tells us that when we call out to God, He inclines His ear. To "incline" one's ear means to concentrate on what's being said. We never have to fight for His attention or direct Him to where we are.

We're God's children and we're precious to Him. Thankfully, He knows that when we're feeling stress, pressure, or pain, we may say things we don't mean. As He concentrates on our words, He also hears the intention of our hearts. When we don't know how to articulate what we need or feel, He understands perfectly. His desire to listen and help is driven by His endless love for us.

But God does more than just lean in. He listens to our cries for help and takes action. This doesn't always mean that He removes what is hurting us, but it does mean that God is with us and will work everything for our good (Romans 8:28).

As we pray today let's remember that God is concentrating on our words. He sees clearly the condition of our hearts and minds. He interprets our words with truth and tenderness. In fact, as you pray, visualize God turning His face to you and bending low to hear.

Make It Personal

When do you most feel like a child fighting for God's attention? What do you want to tell God today?

Today I Bring Praise and Thanksgiving For

Loving Others

Read Psalm 117

Key Verse: 117:2 *His lovingkindness is great toward us.*

ears puddled upon my Bible as I read 1 John 4:7: *Beloved, let us love one another, for love is from God; and everyone who loves is born of God and knows God.*

"I don't hate anyone — I strongly dislike!" I said to God. "They deserve to be hated for the terrible things they've done."

Then my love for God moved me to sorrow, and God began changing my heart. The God of the universe loves me — and you — unconditionally. Who are we to withhold love from others?

I knew what I had to do. John 14:15 clearly explains, *If you love Me, you will keep My commandments.* Loving God means obeying Him. And that means loving all people — even the ones who treat us badly.

Is dumping a wrong attitude possible? Yes. For the believer, there is power to overcome all sin: *By His divine power, God has given us everything we need for living a godly life* (2 Peter 1:3). God has given us everything we need to escape hate.

Maybe you have experienced:

- betrayal of a spouse or best friend
- devastating gossip
- jealousy that led to hate
- a loved one taken or evil that prevailed over justice

These are horrific experiences and God does not overlook evil. God also knows hate is a toxic emotion. For the sake of our health, we must diffuse it. To love people means that we don't wish them any harm. We don't rejoice when they suffer pain or misfortune, and we are not rude to them.

God showed me that the real enemy is Satan who is the mastermind of all evil in this world. Ephesians 6:12 tells us *our struggle is not against flesh and blood, but against the rulers, against the powers, against the world forces of this darkness, against the spiritual forces of wickedness in the heavenly places.* We can transfer our hate to Satan — where it belongs.

After God opened my eyes, my hateful thoughts became less frequent, and over time the hate dissolved completely. There is no evidence that God changed the mean people's hearts. But God changed me.

Make It Personal

How do these verses encourage you? What steps will you take to overcome hate-fillled thoughts?

Today I Bring Praise and Thanksgiving For

Do Not Be Afraid

Read Psalm 118

Key Verse: 118:6 *The Lord is for me; I will not fear; what can man do to me?*

When I was in the fourth grade and living in Livermore, California, I walked home from school. My neighborhood was small and the route I took was safe, but I was afraid of dogs. So, I walked very quickly past homes with dogs, repeating the phrase, "I will not fear," until I was safely in my front yard where my mom waited for me. Those four important words gave me the courage to get home safely.

We all face fearful situations. *I will not fear* should be one of the sweetest, strongest, four words we learn or teach our children. We'll need those words for the rest of our lives.

Common fearful situations include:

- health test results
- loved ones who need salvation
- death
- loss of a job
- financial uncertainties
- the impact of physical storms
- emotional upheaval
- loneliness

In circumstances such as these, we're unable to run away like I ran from the barking dogs. Instead, fear makes us feel like we're trapped in a freezing room, and our body is numb. Fear robs us of sleep and brings tears to our eyes.

God's Word says we needn't be afraid. In Joshua 1:9 we read, *Have I not commanded you? Be strong and courageous! Do not tremble or be dismayed, for the Lord your God is with you wherever you go.* This passage doesn't say that everything will turn out the way we want. But it affirms that God is always with us.

Deuteronomy 31:6 also reminds us, *Be strong and courageous, do not be afraid or tremble at them, [your enemies] for the Lord your God is the one who goes with you. He will not fail you or forsake you.*

I still repeat those precious four words. Often, I repeat them until I feel safe or at peace.

Make It Personal

What is causing you to be fearful at this moment? Which words will you repeat?

Today I Bring Praise and Thanksgiving For

Open My Eyes

Read Psalm 119

Key Verse: 119:18 *Open my eyes, that I may behold wonderful things from Your law.*

Helen Keller said, "The only thing worse than being blind is having sight with no vision."[35] As a blind-deaf woman, Keller's physical vision was non-existent. But she could see and understand in ways many people with good vision cannot. We have physical eyes to see, yet we're blind — living in spiritual darkness, crippled by the inability to perceive God's truth.

Vision and *sight* are defined similarly — both as "the ability to see." When we ask God to open our eyes, we're asking for something more than temporary vision. We're asking for spiritual insight and understanding. Evangelical pastor and author Chuck Swindoll said, "When I think of vision, I have in mind the ability to see above and beyond the majority."[36] To see with spiritual eyes is to understand and reason in ways that aren't natural or visible to human understanding.

When we ask God to open our spiritual eyes, we're asking Him to open our hearts to receive understanding. Then we can:

- discern the truth.
- know the right way.
- gain God's perspective.
- see what He wants us to see.
- obey His Word.

When our spiritual eyes are opened, we can better grasp how wonderful God and His works are. We can understand more fully the wonder of God's laws. In Psalm 119:27 we read, *Make me understand the way of Your precepts, so I will meditate on Your wonders.*

Second Corinthians 4:18 (NLT) tells us, *So we don't look at the troubles we can see now; rather, we fix our gaze on things that cannot be seen. For the things we see now will soon be gone, but the things we cannot see will last forever.* Spiritual sight is our source of strength and hope. Paul wrote in Ephesians 1:18, *I pray that the eyes of your heart may be enlightened, so that you will know what is the hope of His calling.*

Gaining spiritual sight is related directly to how we interact with the Word of God. Let's ask God to open our eyes and the eyes of our loved ones. Then we, like Helen Keller, will have God's spiritual perspective and vision.

Make It Personal

Asking God to open your eyes is a step toward seeing God's perspective. What do you hope to see better?

Today I Bring Praise and Thanksgiving For

When Conflict Arises

Read Psalm 120

Key Verse: 120:1 *In my trouble I cried to the Lord and He answered me.*

Conflict is inevitable. Knowing when and how to engage requires wisdom.

When to engage:

- Proverbs 26:4 tells us, *Do not answer a fool according to his folly, or you will also be like him.* Not every conflict or heated discussion needs to be addressed.

- Pray for wisdom to know when to engage and when to disregard. Once, a woman who had different religious views from me attacked me for my beliefs. The conversation hurt, and when she wasn't looking, I cried. Because I saw this woman on a regular basis, I spent time in prayer and Bible reading to discern what to do. I felt God leading me to stay quiet since arguing wouldn't have benefited me or her.

How to engage:

- Resist the urge to impulsively engage in conversation. First, pray for wisdom and understanding, for the right words to use, for God to prepare the other person's heart, and for the right timing.

- When the time is right, James 1:19 says, *Be quick to hear, slow to speak and slow to anger.* Note that James is writing to Christians. The devil can take "good people" in "good places" and create conflict.

- Prepare to listen, with the intent to understand. Proverbs 10:19 warns, *When there are many words, transgression is unavoidable, but he who restrains his lips is wise.* Choose words carefully and calmly. Before the conversation begins, imagine that Jesus sits in a nearby chair.

- Ask God to reveal our part in the conflict or fault. Conflict could be caused by miscommunication, lack of knowledge, or a sinful attitude. Pray for strength to do what is right. Forgive and ask to be forgiven as appropriate.

Conflict might tie knots in our stomach or make us cry but it doesn't have to end badly. God uses conflict to teach us so we'll grow into spiritually mature Christians. God can bring resolution, heal our hearts, or say it's okay to walk away. Regardless of the outcome, hang onto the lesson.

Make It Personal

Reflect on a past or current conflict. How did or does God direct you to handle it?

Today I Bring Praise and Thanksgiving For

Something About These Mountains

Read Psalm 121

Key Verses: 121:1–2 *I will lift up my eyes to the mountains; from where shall my help come? My help comes from the LORD, who made heaven and earth.*

I jerked on my hiking boots and ran out the door. My friend was waiting for me to begin our hike in the mountains. We met at the bottom of the trail and started the five-mile trek to the top. Bottled waters in my backpack increased the weight I was carrying. But that's not all that was weighing on me.

Anguish about a loved one's choices hurt my heart.

Fog hung low on the cool, damp morning, and I felt small amid the tall evergreens.

At the top of the mountain we watched the fog dissipate as the sun broke through to reveal a clear, blue sky. Standing on a rock, I saw the valley below and the distant mountain ranges. Again, I felt small.

But the spectacular mountains also reminded me of their Creator. A surge of strength compelled me to lift my hands to heaven and cry out, "God help me!" Tears filled my eyes and then slipped down my face.

My words echoed across the canyons. Then complete silence.

Something about the majestic Blue Ridge Mountains always

reminds me of God's power. David once asked, *Who may ascend into the hill of the Lord? And who may stand in His holy place?* (Psalm 24:3).

When we're weighed down with despair and fog fills our mind, we can look to God for help. The same God who created the mountains will help us with everything we need. Stand on that rock-solid truth.

Make It Personal

What area of your life do you need to take to the mountaintop and release? What burden is weighing you down?

Praise and Thanksgiving:

Prosperity

Read Psalm 122

Key Verse: 122:6 *Pray for the peace of Jerusalem: May they prosper who love you.*

sk a group of people their definition of *prosperity* and their response will probably be "material possessions and wealth." Sometimes that is what prosperity means. But in the context of this psalm, the Hebrew word translated *prosper* means to be "secure, tranquil, and at rest."

Those who love Zion — the city that loves and serves God — will prosper with peace. Prosperity, then, refers to being rich with peace in all situations. We can also have peace within our conscience when choosing between right and wrong.

Wiersbe describes prosperity as "spiritual enrichment."[37] Those who prosper in peace have been spiritually enriched. Peace comes as we become more aware of the character of God, His power, and the significance of His Son's sacrifice.

By investing in spiritual matters our lives are dramatically enriched. How do we invest?

- We spend time with God in prayer. We tell Him how we really feel. We ask Him to reveal Himself to us personally.

- We read the Bible. Getting to know God is the most significant thing we can do to change our lives — to find prosperity, security, hope. We need to pray before reading the Bible and ask God to help us understand and apply His words. We can't know what we don't read. We prosper because we have access to God's very words.

- We get involved in a Bible study group. It's helpful to have others to study with.
- We find a Bible-believing church. Worshipping with others brings glory to God. But worship and lessons from the Bible also provide strength, inspiration, and encouragement for a new week. Becoming involved — even serving in one capacity or another — produces a natural high.

We may prosper with material possessions, but the greatest prosperity is our security and peace with God. These can never be taken from us.

Make It Personal

How would you define prosperity? Do you consider yourself prosperous? Why or why not?

Today I Bring Praise and Thanksgiving For

Cultivating Our Minds

Read Psalm 123

Key Verse: 123:1 *To You I lift my eyes, O You who are enthroned in the heavens!*

Weeds grow naturally, but we must cultivate a flower garden. Time, attention, and nourishment are required to grow beautiful flowers. Without them, weeds take over.

A life is like a flower garden. To produce something lovely, we must make time to lift our eyes to our Creator so He can nourish our souls. Otherwise, weeds will take over.

Romans 8:6 tells us, *The mind set on the flesh is death, but the mind set on the Spirit is life.*

Many TV programs show us how the world thinks. Look at these examples:

- You're watching a drama. The woman in an adulterous affair appears to be having fun, wrapped up in the romance of a new or mysterious love. You become envious, wishing your own husband could be that romantic.

- You're viewing a commercial, but the intended message is missed because you're focused on the exceptional home filled with an array of appliances and expensive décor. You deserve that too, and regardless of the cost, you won't be satisfied until you get it.

- You're watching a reality TV show, and the women laugh as they talk negatively about someone. Gossip seems funny, harmless — nothing to feel guilty about.

Romans 12:2 warns, *Do not be conformed to this world, but be transformed by the renewing of your mind.* An unknown author once said: "Watch your thoughts for they become words. Watch your words for they become actions. Watch your actions for they become habits. Watch your habits, for they become your character. And watch your character, for it becomes your destiny!" What we think, we become.

We renew our minds by regularly pulling the weeds of sinful thoughts before they take root, grow tall, and strangle the flowers. Second Corinthians 10:5 teaches that we tend our garden by *taking every thought captive to the obedience of Christ.* In other words, we spend time in God's Word, give God our thoughts, and allow His thoughts to nourish our bodies so we can grow.

The result? *The Lord will continually guide you . . . and you will be like a watered garden* (Isaiah 58:11).

Make It Personal

Which area in your spiritual garden most needs to be cultivated?

Today I Bring Praise and Thanksgiving For

God Is on Our Side

Read Psalm 124

Key Verse: 124:2 *Had it not been for the Lord who was on our side.*

Most of us can recall being chosen — or not chosen — on the ball team at recess while in elementary school. How long we waited influenced how valuable we thought we were.

God has chosen us already, and when we say "yes" to Him, we step over to His team. From that moment on, God is on our side. Mark 9:40 tells us this truth: *For He who is not against us is for us.* This is repeated in Romans 8:31: *If God is for us, who is against us?*

Sometimes, when the storm clouds roll in and prayers go unanswered, we don't feel like God is on our side. We may wonder if God's in the field with the better players. When we're chastised with His strong hand of discipline, we may get the impression that God is mad and has turned away.

But this isn't true.

When we were children, we didn't like experiencing consequences for our actions, but we knew our parents still loved us. As parents or guardians, we don't enjoy dishing out discipline, but we strive to correct with the hope that our children will become successful, productive adults.

As God shapes us, it can feel like harsh discipline. When God seems to prevent the very things we're striving for, it can appear He's against us. But Proverbs 3:12 assures us, *The Lord cor-*

rects those He loves, just as a father corrects a child in whom he delights (NLT).

God's correction is helpful, not detrimental. His discipline trains us and brings us closer to Him. Hebrews 12:7 tells us, *It is for discipline that you endure; God deals with you as with sons; for what son is there whom his father does not discipline?*

God has chosen us, and each of us is a valuable child on His team. He is always on our side — especially during the painful times of correction. Remember and recite the phrase: God is on my side. Repeat it now. Repeat it often.

Make It Personal

Has there ever been a time you thought God was against you? What was the outcome?

Today I Bring Praise and Thanksgiving For

Surrounded

Read Psalm 125

Key Verse: 125:2 *As the mountains surround Jerusalem, so the Lord surrounds His people from this time forth and forever.*

*P*icture in your mind a town surrounded by mountains. To get to the town you have to hike steep hills. Or drive sharp inclines to pass through it. You not only see the towering mountains, but you experience their presence. You smell the fragrant evergreens. You feel small in comparison and yet protected.

That is how God surrounds His people.

With God we're totally encircled, enveloped, and hemmed in. That's God's covering on us.

We may feel surrounded by a hostile work environment, negative people, deception, pain, and suffering. And perhaps we are. Technology — however skewed — has allowed us to view our surroundings and our entire world. We're witness to chaos, heartache, and financial instability. Sometimes we might feel traumatized, wobbly, or knocked down for a brief time. But God will enable us to get back up, stand firm in our faith, and believe Him when He says He ultimately surrounds us.

In Psalm 139:5 we read, *You have enclosed me behind and before, and laid Your hand upon me.*

Look to every direction — God is there. He has our back, our front, and our top too.

God goes before us. Anything that gets through to us, comes

through Him. Whatever it is — good or bad — God has a purpose. He will use what the enemy intended for bad and make it good.

Today's key verse reminds us that God surrounds us with Himself: His love, favor, mercy, and power. Will we open our hearts and hands to receive this gift? Today, let's trust God as He envelops us like the powerful mountains wrap themselves around a small town.

Make It Personal

When have you felt God's strong presence surrounding you?

Today I Bring Praise and Thanksgiving For

Sowing and Reaping

Read Psalm 126

Key Verse: 126:5 *Those who sow in tears shall reap with a joyful shouting.*

Have you ever cried all day? Have you ever asked, *Why does life have to be so hard?* How often do you feel that way?

The word *sow* in our key verse may remind you of the farmer who sows seeds months before he reaps a harvest.

John Piper wrote, [A] "field needs to be sowed. That is the way life is. I do not feel like it, but I will take my bag of seeds and go out in the fields and do my crying while I do my duty. I will sow in tears. If you do that, the promise of the psalm is that 'you will reap with shouts of joy.' "[37]

Sowing in tears could refer to the hard work associated with any job we do or attitude we have.

- For a farmer, physical exertion is required as he plows through fierce weather.

- The businesswoman may need grace to respond in a Christlike manner to a ferocious group of colleagues.

- Tears may represent a repentant heart, crying over sin.

- Frequently, our tears reflect a broken heart as we pray for those who need to turn their hearts to God.

Galatians 6:9 reminds us, *Let us not lose heart in doing good, for in due time we will reap if we do not grow weary.*

You may have hardship and pain but persevere in prayer and you'll see the joyful harvest. You'll be stronger in faith, trust God more, and rely on Him to change your heart and mind — and the hearts of others.

Our tears and difficulties won't last forever, *so be strong and do not give up, for your work will be rewarded* (2 Chronicles 15:7).

Make It Personal

When has God brought a joyful harvest after you've sown in tears?

Today I Bring Praise and Thanksgiving For

Building and Protecting

Read Psalm 127

Key Verse: 127:1 *Unless the Lord builds the house, they labor in vain who build it.*

*I*n fourth grade, I used sugar cubes to build a replica of one of the beautiful Old California Missions. When the day arrived to take in our projects, I proudly carried mine to school. But when I moved one of my hands from the cardboard foundation to open the door to the school, I dropped my mission, and it broke into pieces. Thankfully, my teacher helped me put the mission back together piece by piece. It didn't look like the original, but my teacher envisioned its prior loveliness and the hard work that went into creating it. I had worked for weeks, but my masterpiece crumbled in two seconds.

Unlike my fourth-grade project, what God builds lasts and is significant. We're not supposed to build anything on our own — for the outcome is failure.

God has empowered us to build our homes, churches, and communities. Whether we're building with steel to create buildings or with love to build lives, we need God's help.

Nehemiah 4:14 reminds us, *Fight for your brothers, your sons, your daughters, your wives and your houses.* Whether we think we know what to do, or we haven't a clue, turn to God and allow Him to build that which will endure.

We must diligently pray Lamentations 2:19: *Rise during the night and cry out. Pour out your hearts like water to the Lord. Lift up your hands to Him in prayer, pleading for your children, for in every street they are faint with hunger* (NLT). Many children are starved for the truth of God. Some are weary, like we are, facing huge obstacles while trying to live for God.

We can pray as David did in 1 Chronicles 29:19: *Give to my son Solomon a perfect heart to keep Your commandments, Your testimonies and Your statutes, and to do them all, and to build the temple, for which I have made provision.*

It's never a waste of time to pray for our families. Dr. Charles Stanley wrote, "You cannot get involved in a wiser or more everlasting venture than pouring your spiritual wealth into another person's mind and heart."[39] Are we pouring into our loved ones?

Make It Personal

How are you building your home? Is it with sugar cubes or with the power of God's hand?

Today I Bring Praise and Thanksgiving For

Obedience Isn't Always Easy

Read Psalm 128

Key Verse: 128:1 *How blessed is everyone who fears the Lord, who walks in His ways.*

Obeying God is easy when we agree with God's plan or it suits our purpose. But what if obedience is costly, illogical, or inconvenient? Ellie shares her story of obedience:

> I became a Christian at a young age. After one failed marriage, my eight-year-old son and I moved in with my new boyfriend. I tried to explain my living arrangement to God — to justify that financially this made sense. But I felt a disconnection. Sin stood as a wall. Then one day my boyfriend and I decided to be obedient and do what's right. We moved into separate dwellings, then got married. Immediately, peace flooded into my body! Although we had gone about things backwards, God showed compassion and forgave us. For the first time in a long time, I felt I was in a right relationship with God. But then God blessed us even more. After eight years of wishing for another child, we received the news that a new baby was on the way!

God knows life is better when we live within His boundaries and walk in His ways. He doesn't want anything standing between us and Him.

Deuteronomy 30:9–11 tell us, *Then the Lord your God will prosper you abundantly in all the work of your hand, in the offspring of your body ... for the Lord will again rejoice over you for good, just as He rejoiced over your fathers; obey the Lord your God to keep His commandments and His statutes which are written in this book of the law, if you turn to the Lord your God with all your heart and soul. For this commandment which I command you today is not too difficult for you, nor is it out of reach.*

God will help us do what seems impossible to do on our own. When we desire to obey, He provides us with strength to do what He asks. Oh, how delighted God must be when we choose to leave our comfort zone and step out in faith to obey!

Our part is to obey God. His part is to handle the outcome.

Make It Personal

What does obeying God look like for you? Refraining from a sinful habit? Loving the undeserving? Praying for your enemy? Or something else?

Today I Bring Praise and Thanksgiving For

He Has

Read Psalm 129

Key Verse: 129:4 *The Lord is righteous; He has cut in two the cords of the wicked.*

God haters and evildoers exist. Terrorist attacks and crimes that target select people groups, painfully remind us of modern-day evil. Christians are among those under attack. The psalmist wrote that God's people would never be destroyed. Still, the church has been persecuted for centuries.

Recently I saw the movie, *Paul, Apostle of Christ.* Christians were tortured as their bodies were literally ripped apart by lions in a place called Nero's Circus. There, too, Christians were tied to stakes and set on fire to light the city. Fortunately, the movie didn't include such graphic scenes of torture.

I keep replaying the words Luke spoke to them in their dank cells before they were led to their horrible deaths: "It will hurt for a moment — then you will be with Jesus in heaven forever." They gripped hands and a smile spread across their faces, signifying a brief moment of comfort and joy.

In the accounts of violence and torture recorded in Scripture, there aren't many inspirational thoughts we can gather like flowers put into vases to bring us joy when we look on their beauty. We take no pleasure in reading or hearing about the horrendous torture of any Jew or Christian — then or now.

First-century believers endured excruciating persecution for the sake of Christ. And yet our key verse tells us that God has

263

cut in two the cords of the wicked. *He has*. Not *He will*. But He has *already* conquered.

Cords were used to fasten the plow to the ox when plowing. The wicked mentioned in our key verse schemed to plow over Zion and destroy God's people. But they couldn't separate God's people from Him — not then, and not now. *He has* is an indication of what is to come — *He has* already devised a plan and won the victory.

- *He has* promised that the wicked won't prevail.
- *He has* brought us out of persecution.
- *He has* assured us that we'll be with Him in eternity.
- *He has* not ignored our suffering or been indifferent to our wailing.

Here are flowers of inspiration: We can have joy, not fear. We can trust the God who has already declared Himself the victor.

Make It Personal

What can you do when you feel persecuted for being a Christian?

Today I Bring Praise and Thanksgiving For

Watchwoman

Read Psalm 130

Key Verse: 130:6 *My soul waits for the Lord more than watchmen for the morning; indeed, more than watchmen for the morning.*

*I*n ancient times, a watchman's job was critical. Some watchmen were positioned in towers to guard the crops from animals or thieves. Others mounted the city's walls to serve as lookouts. If an adversary approached, watchmen sounded the alarm and closed the gates. Watchmen surveyed their surroundings and eagerly waited for the morning. Their nights were long, but the morning was always certain.

Onlooker, careful watcher, defender, or guard — all words used to describe a watchman. Are we as watchful?

Our key verse tells us the writer of this psalm waited for the Lord more than the watchmen wait for the morning. As "watchwomen," we eagerly wait and watch for the return of our Lord Jesus.

Jesus told the parable about being prepared and watching for the Lord's return. Ten virgins were watching for the bridegroom's arrival. They took their lamps and went out to meet the bridegroom. Five were wise and took jars of extra oil with them. Five foolish ones didn't take enough oil. The wise ones were ready — they had prepared. When the bridegroom arrived in the middle of the night, the wise ones went in to the banquet and the door was shut (Matthew 25:1–13).

What does this have to do with Jesus' return? Jesus Christ

is called the bridegroom of the church and one day He will return (Ephesians 5:25–32). Are we prepared for His return? Ultimately, we're ready when we receive Christ as Savior. (See "Righteous Judgment," Psalm 98 for steps to accepting Jesus Christ as Savior.)

No one knows the hour Christ will return, so we must always be ready with eyes fixed on Him at all times. The virgins were sleeping. We might be working, eating, or relaxing. But what we're doing doesn't matter as long as we're prepared, not needing to scurry to make things right.

Let's fill our lamps with extra oil, face the horizon, and keep watching.

Make It Personal

In what ways are you preparing for Christ's return? In what ways are you keeping watch?

Today I Bring Praise and Thanksgiving For

Quiet Hope

Read Psalm 131

Key Verses: 131:2–3 *Surely I have composed and quieted my soul; like a weaned child rests against his mother, my soul is like a weaned child within me. O Israel, hope in the Lord from this time forth and forever.*

The picture of Jesus with children we sometimes see in books is undeniably beautiful. In Matthew 18:3, when the apostles are arguing about who is the greatest, Jesus reaches for a small child. I envision Jesus picking up the child and setting her on His lap. Her eyes meet His and they sparkle with delight. A smile emerges across both their faces. The child then, leans her head on His chest and wraps her arms around His neck, as if to say, "I'm completely safe in my Father's arms."

When we're around small children, we see their trusting nature. Children don't work out the details of their fears or problems on their own — they trust their parents to care for them and to provide for what they need. And you know what? Sometimes children don't know what they need. They depend on their caregiver's knowledge.

Once a toddler is weaned, she moves on to solid food. We're like that small child, and our solid food is confident hope in our divine caregiver — hope that frees us from fear.

James Burton Coffman wrote that it's a " 'weaned child' not a nursing child that is mentioned [in our key verse].[40] The point is that the human soul needs weaning from all of its anxious

267

ambitions, before it can enjoy the tranquility of a heart in tune with God's will. The psalmist . . . affirms that he is indeed weaned from such hurtful things."

A child's heart is peaceful and satisfied when she's wrapped safely in her father's arms. We can be like that child when we view God as our loving parent and place our hope in Him.

We need to build every part of our life on the hope we have in God. Then we, like David, will say as he did in our key verse, *"I have stilled and quieted my soul"* (NIV).

Make It Personal

How will you find time to be quiet and still before God today? What makes you or your thoughts move at a rapid pace?

Today I Bring Praise and Thanksgiving For

Daily Provision

Read Psalm 132

Key Verse: 132:15 *I will abundantly bless her provision; I will satisfy her needy with bread.*

A single woman, raising children on a salary from a minimum wage job, is in an undeniably difficult situation. I watched my mother live that reality. I witnessed the emotional and physical tolls it took on her.

Our situation seemed bleak. But decades later, I see how God provided. In many ways, we flourished spiritually. For example, when there was no money for rent or a good meal, I listened to my mother weep and then cry out to God to meet our needs. My mom had what some people don't — a deep dependence on God. Today, I am rich with the knowledge that God satisfies — even exceeds — our needs, whether they be physical, mental, emotional, or spiritual.

The Bible tells us in Philippians 4:19, *My God will supply all your needs according to His riches in glory in Christ Jesus.*

- When we have a financial need. God's provision can come through work, friends, family, and church organizations. *Psalm 107:9 tells us, He has satisfied the thirsty soul, and the hungry soul He has filled with what is good.* When I was a child, for example, an anonymous person paid for me to attend week-long church camps.

- When we're weak. Second Corinthians 12:9 tells us, *[The Lord] has said to me, "My grace is sufficient for you, for power is perfected in weakness." Most gladly, therefore, I will rather boast about my weaknesses, so that the power of Christ may dwell in me.* Despite working two jobs and battling fatigue, my mother remained strong. God provided her with everything she needed.

- When we need more than temporary bread. Jesus said in John 6:35, *I am the bread of life; he who comes to Me will not hunger, and he who believes in Me will never thirst.* God provides a way for us to have everlasting life — the greatest provision of all.

Romans 8:32 provides encouragement: *He who did not spare His own Son, but delivered Him over for us all, how will He not also with Him freely give us all things?*

Reflecting on the good things God has provided in the past, gives us hope for provision in the future.

Make It Personal

In what way do you need God's provision today?

Today I Bring Praise and Thanksgiving For

Unity

Read Psalm 133

Key Verse: 133:1 *Behold, how good and pleasant it is for brothers to dwell together in unity!*

My friends Huritika and Sudha were both born and raised in India. They have never traveled beyond its borders. I live on the other side of the world from them. I met them when I was part of a small group that visited one of the Indian schools. Although we're teachers, we're extraordinarily different in all visible ways: appearance, finances, ethnicity, habits, social rules, fashion, schedules, and disciplines.

But there is one thing — invisible at first — that makes us the same. We are Christ-followers and have chosen to love and serve only Him all our lives. Because of this one similarity, we are bonded in unity.

More often, though, cultural differences lead to quarrels. This is also true within the church: The thread that should bind us together becomes shredded by perceived judgments. Some Christ-followers are divisive with their brothers and sisters in Christ. They might be easily offended, hateful, or judgmental. Onlookers want to get as far away as possible.

Addressing Christians, James asked, *What causes fights and quarrels among you? Don't they come from your desires that battle within you?* (James 4:1 NIV). He said their fighting was the result of envy, selfish ambition, arrogance, and independence. These attitudes don't leave much room for unity.

Galatians 5:17 tells us, *The flesh sets its desire against the Spirit, and the Spirit against the flesh; for these are in opposition to one another so that you may not do the things that you please.* When our human desires (our flesh) oppose the Spirit who resides in us, the result is unrest and stress. Being at war with the Spirit leads to an unhappy disposition. And people who quarrel with themselves quarrel with others too.

Our brothers and sisters in Christ come from all cultures and nations. We may have cultural differences, but we're unified by our mutual love for Jesus Christ

Weirsbe tells us, "Externals divide us . . . while the Spirit brings us together . . . ."[41] Unity isn't something we create. It comes from God — when hearts are turned toward Him.

Make It Personal

Are you currently quarrelling? If yes, what do you think is the root cause? If no, what keeps you unified with others?

Today I Bring Praise and Thanksgiving For

Service That Blesses God

Read Psalm 134

Key Verse: 134:1 *Behold, bless the Lord, all servants of the Lord, who serve by night in the house of the Lord!*

The doorbell rang. When I opened the door, there stood Beverly, grinning from ear to ear. In her hands, she held several baskets. I invited her in and helped her carry the load to the kitchen. Beverly had brought a beautiful, colorful array of food: homemade chili, buttery cornbread, baked spaghetti, green salad with chunks of red tomatoes, loaves of bakery bread, bananas, apples, oranges, and brownies!

She said, "Your life is overflowing with hardship so I figured your plate should be too."

Beverly saw my need and met it.

We bless the Lord when we serve the people He loves. And by helping others, we ultimately serve God. Matthew 25:40 tells us, *Truly I say to you, to the extent that you did it to one of these brothers of Mine, even the least of them, you did it to Me.*

We can serve others in a hundred ways. For starters, we can:

- provide financially for the sick or hurting or buy someone's lunch.
- make food, send cards, sew clothes, or knit gloves.
- listen to someone who's heartbroken or lonely.
- sing or teach in church; greet and welcome others.

- volunteer to share your hobby, talent, or skill.
- babysit the young or elderly.

In Acts 9:36 we read about Dorcas: *Now in Joppa there was a disciple named Tabitha (which translated in Greek is called Dorcas); this woman was abounding with deeds of kindness and charity which she continually did.* Her kindness and charitable deeds make her a stand-out gal. For example, she sewed tunics and garments for widows.

Beverly and Dorcus blessed God by serving others. We're all busy. We may be in need ourselves. But Proverbs 11:25 tells us, *He who waters will himself be watered.* The same verse in the NIV says, *Whoever refreshes others will be refreshed.* Bless God, serve others, and be refreshed.

Make It Personal

What is your favorite way to bless God? In what other ways not listed above could you serve others?

Today I Bring Praise and Thanksgiving For

What's in a Name?

Read Psalm 135

Key Verse: 135:13 *Your name, O Lord, is everlasting, Your remembrance, O Lord, throughout all generations.*

Choosing a baby's name is a huge undertaking. Some go for popular or cute. Many choose family names. Others study the meaning behind a name and select one based on that. When we're adults researching where our name originates is interesting. Names are important.

God has many names. Fully comprehending who He is impacts who we are. Let's take a look at some of the names of God:

Almighty - Revelation 1:8
Alpha - Revelation 1:8
Comforter - Jeremiah 8:18
Emmanuel - Matthew 1:23
Friend of Sinners - Matthew 11:19
Guide - Psalm 48:14
I Am - Exodus 3:14
Jesus - Matthew 1:21
Light of the World - John 8:12
Lord of Lords - 1 Timothy 6:15
Messiah - John 1:41
Omega - Revelation 1:8
Prince of Peace - Isaiah 9:6
Refiner - Malachi 3:2
Rock - Deuteronomy 32:4
Wonderful Counselor - Isaiah 9:6
Lion of the Tribe of Judah - Revelation 5:5

King of Kings - 1 Timothy 6:15
The Christ - Matthew 1:16
Deliverer - Romans 11:26
Everlasting Father - Isaiah 9:6
Good Shepherd - John 10:11
High Priest - Hebrews 3:1
Jehovah - Psalm 83:18
Lamb of God - John 1:29
Bridegroom - Matthew 9:15
Master - Matthew 23:8
Mighty God - Isaiah 9:6
Physician - Matthew 9:12
Redeemer - Isaiah 41:14
Refuge - Isaiah 25:4
Savior - Luke 1:47
Righteousness - Jeremiah 23:6

And there are more. This list only begins to show us who God is. He is our Father forever, and we are His children and His inheritance. Kids of the King. Chosen and adopted. Endlessly loved.

That's what's in a name.

Let's declare our identity and live like we believe it.

Make It Personal

Which name of God means the most to you in your current season of life?

Today I Bring Praise and Thanksgiving For

Lovingkindness

Read Psalm 136

Key Verse: 136:1 *Give thanks to the Lord, for He is good, for His lovingkindness is everlasting.*

*D*o you ever feel like you've reached your limit with God's mercy allowance? Or have you thought that past rebellion led you to do things outside of God's plan, and He couldn't possibly still love you?

In this single psalm, we're told twenty-six times that God loves us forever. Bible translations use the words *lovingkindness, steadfast love* or *faithful love,* but the KJV and the NKJV both use the word *mercy.* Bible commentator Matthew Henry writes, "By 'mercy' we understand the Lord's disposition to save those whom sin has rendered miserable."[42]

Miserable might sound strange but that's what we'd be without God's love. We don't have to wonder if we're worthy of His love because Romans 5:8 tells us how He proved His love: *God demonstrates His own love toward us, in that while we were yet sinners, Christ died for us.* Christ died so we could live with Him forever.

God's love and mercy drove Him to give us His Son, Jesus Christ. This perfect love is freely lavished on all people and will never be withdrawn.

The Greek word for God's love is *agape.* This love is a sacrificial commitment — not the kind of love that is based on emotional feelings. His is a promised love, regardless if we're unlovable. In fact, none of us deserves His love, but we receive it because, as 1 John 4:8 tells us, *Everything about God is love and everything He does pours forth from love.* Love is His nature.

God has done His part. What's left is our part: We can refuse God's love or we can choose to believe there isn't anything we can do that would motivate God to retract His love. He loves us and longs to be kind and merciful forever.

Choose to believe Ephesians 2:4–5: *God, being rich in mercy, because of His great love with which He loved us, even when we were dead in our transgressions, made us alive together with Christ.* Choose God's love and become alive again.

Make It Personal

How has God shown His love, mercy, and kindness recently?

Today I Bring Praise and Thanksgiving For

Letting Go of the Past

Read Psalm 137

Key Verse: 137:1 *By the rivers of Babylon, there we sat down and wept, when we remembered Zion.*

She came to draw water during the hot part of the day. Maybe she wanted to be alone; maybe she was fearful of snickers and gossip. Her past followed her. She'd been married five times and was now living with a man who wasn't her husband.

Then she met Jesus. He offered her forgiveness for the past. She accepted and immediately became an evangelist (John 4:1-42).

Jesus freed this Samaritan woman from her past. Her sin no longer held her captive.

The writer of Psalm 137 also had a past. As a former exile he wrote about his painful memories. As we reflect on our past, we might have painful memories too. They may flood us with unwarranted guilt. And that's what Satan wants — to remind us of our past sin so we feel unworthy — too unworthy to be of any use to God.

If you have confessed your sins, cling to the words of Isaiah 43:18–19: *Do not call to mind the former things, or ponder things of the past. Behold, I will do something new.*

If there's unconfessed sin that weighs heavy on your heart, think on 1 John 1:9: *If we confess our sins, He is faithful and righteous to forgive us our sins and to cleanse us from all unrighteousness.*

Then choose to believe 2 Corinthians 5:17: *If anyone is in*

Christ, he is a new creature; the old things passed away; behold, new things have come.

When we accept God's gift of salvation, we become new people, completely worthy and accepted by God. And just like the Samaritan woman, we've been freed from the bondage of our past. Our chains have been removed and we have new freedom in Christ. Forget the guilt. Remember our faithful God.

Make It Personal

Is anything keeping you in bondage? Do you sometimes think your past disqualifies you from serving God? Why or why not?

Today I Bring Praise and Thanksgiving For

God's Plan for You

Read Psalm 138

Key Verse: 138:8 *The Lord will accomplish what concerns me.*

How does God accomplish His plan and purpose for each one of us?

God is mysterious. We can't always know with one-hundred percent surety exactly what we should do. But that doesn't change this significant, life-changing truth found in Jeremiah 29:11 (NIV): *"I know the plans I have for you," declares the Lord, "plans to prosper you and not to harm you, plans to give you hope and a future."*

No matter what our age or our season of life, God has plans for us. He desires us to be willing participants in the execution of those plans. He wants us to know His will and follow in it. Why? Because His plans are good.

Isaiah 46:10 says, *My purpose will be established and I will accomplish all My good pleasure. Established* is defined as "bringing into existence." *Accomplish* is similar in meaning: "to bring to completion."

Established and accomplished are used in the context of God's care for your life. How does that make you feel?

God has equipped each of us with unique talents, desires, and abilities that enable us to do His will. He works through circumstances and events. He uses people around us to encourage us. He puts within our hearts the burning passion and motivation necessary to do His will. Our life is a puzzle, and each of these gifts is a piece of that puzzle.

God has a marvelous plan. What is our part to bring it to fruition?

We begin by cultivating our relationship with God through prayer, Bible reading, and spending time with others who are growing in Christ. In due time, we'll be more familiar with God's ways. Experiences will teach us to have a deeper trust. The closer we become to God, the more our desires will align with His desires for us. Make God a part of every decision and acknowledge Him. Proverbs 3:6 tells us, *In all your ways acknowledge Him, and He will make your paths straight.* In other words, He'll show us the way to go.

We do what we believe God has called us to do, and we leave the results to Him. We can be confident that God will execute His plans when we allow Him to do so.

Make It Personal

How is your life affected by God's promise in Jeremiah 29:11? What do you believe God is calling you to do in this season of life?

Today I Bring Praise and Thanksgiving For

More Than Sand

Read Psalm 139

Key Verses: 139:17–18 *How precious also are your thoughts to me, O God! How vast the sum of them! If I should count them, they would outnumber the sand.*

Picture yourself on a beach at sunrise. Pink, yellow, orange, and purple blend across the sky. The ocean is calm, its surface like shiny glass as the sun's rays reflect on it. Your eyes look to the never-ending horizon, and you wonder what is on the other side.

You glance to your right. People walk along the shoreline. Some children frolic in the waves. To your left, pet owners toss a Frisbee to their dogs. On the highest point along the beach sits a sandcastle, that survived the evening's high tide. The sand extends as far as you can see to the right and to the left.

Scientist Robert Krulwich reports, "If you assume a grain of sand has an average size, and you calculate how many grains are in a teaspoon and then multiply by all the beaches and deserts in the world, the Earth has roughly (and we're speaking *very* roughly here) 7.5×10^{18} grains of sand, or seven quintillion, five hundred quadrillion grains."[43]

I can't even write that number. The point is, when God says His thoughts about us are more numerous than the sand on the beaches, He's declaring He thinks about us a whole lot. The thought is unfathomable. But try to wrap your mind around that fact for a few minutes.

The intentional statement made by Sovereign God in our key verse is so profound that it requires an incredible amount of faith to take Him at His word. When He says He thinks about us, He means He never takes a break.

We can live well today and sleep soundly tonight. God is thinking about us and about every single thing that concerns us.

Make It Personal

What is the hardest part of believing God thinks about you this much?

Today I Bring Praise and Thanksgiving For

An Extraordinary Response

Read Psalm 140

Key Verse: 140:4 *Keep me, O Lord, from the hands of the wicked; preserve me from violent men who have purposed to trip up my feet.*

*D*o we stand out as different in our response to people? Or do we fit into the world's idea of how we're expected to respond?

David was asking God for protection from his troubles . . . again. At the time David wrote this psalm, he was likely one of King Saul's staff. The other members of his staff spread lies and set traps to sabotage David, who was a good man. This still occurs today. Often, we're the target of wicked people who desire to bring trouble on God's people. But David shows us how to respond to trouble like this.

David had the ability and opportunity to kill Saul. But he chose not to. The story plays out in 1 Samuel 24:

- King Saul had been searching for David. He didn't know David was hiding in a cave when he entered. David crept slowly towards Saul and used his sword to cut off a section of his robe, but spared his life. Feeling ashamed that he'd disrespected the king, David said, *My lord and king! . . . then bowed himself to the ground* (v. 8).

- David asked King Saul, *Why do you listen to [the lies] of the men?* (v. 9). He explained that he could've killed Saul but he chose to leave Saul's fate in God's hands (vv. 11-12).

- Then Saul wept. He said, *You are more righteous than I; for you have dealt well with me, while I dealt wickedly with you* (vv. 16-17).

- Saul ended by saying, *I know that you will surely be king and that the kingdom of Israel will be established in your hand* (v. 20).

Is this how we respond to people who heap trouble on us? Do we resist retaliation on those who lie? Do we allow God to intervene with justice and vengeance of His choosing?

David is our example:
- to live worthy so others see God in us and are drawn to Him

- to love and respect others

- to win others for Christ because we stand out as different

- to refuse payback

David didn't respond in ordinary ways. Rather, extraordinarily. And because the Holy Spirit resides in us, we can respond in extraordinary ways too.

Make It Personal

How will you use David's example in future situations?

Today I Bring Praise and Thanksgiving For

Friendship That Matters

Read Psalm 141

Key Verse: 141:8 *My eyes are toward You, O God, the Lord; in You I take refuge; do not leave me defenseless.*

Have you heard about those relationship sites on the Internet where people can specify the kind of companionship they're seeking? What David wrote in these ten verses would sound like one of these advertisements.

> MAN SEEKING SOMEONE TO: Listen to me, help me spurn sin, defend my actions, assist in guarding my mouth, remind me of hope, train me in new concepts, help me keep my eyes focused, help me discern, teach me to avoid snares from my enemies, help me plan, strategize along beside me, and enable me to walk safely.

In short, David asked for accountability. He wanted God to steer him away from evil and to surround him with righteous friends.

God doesn't leave us defenseless. He gave us a valuable gift — the treasured gift of friendship. The Bible unmistakably outlines the role of a godly friend:

- Godly friends enhance each other's lives. Their words encourage us in hardship and offer support for our dreams. They listen when we suffer and celebrate our joy. Proverbs 27:17 tells us, *Iron sharpens iron, so one man sharpens another.*

- Godly friends share Christian values that hold us accountable. This friend won't agree out of fear she'll hurt our feelings. Sometimes a godly friend's convicting words sting, but Proverbs 27:6 tells us, *Faithful are the wounds of a friend.*

- Godly friends counsel each other. Proverbs 19:20 tells us, *Listen to counsel and accept discipline, that you may be wise the rest of your days.*

- Godly friends love unconditionally. They don't avoid us or abandon us when we're suffering. Proverbs 17:17 tells us, *A friend loves at all times, and a brother is born for adversity.*

- Godly friends believe that prayer is a powerful weapon and use it to fight for each other. Ephesians 6:18 (NLT) tells us, *Pray in the Spirit at all times and on every occasion. Stay alert and be persistent in your prayers for all believers everywhere.*

Thank You, God, for blessing us with friends. Help us find friends like this — and be that friend too.

Make It Personal

What would your friend request look like? Do you have a true friend who holds you accountable?

Today I Bring Praise and Thanksgiving For

Run to the Cave

Read Psalm 142

Key Verse: 142:5 *You are my refuge.*

Overwhelmed with pain and despair, David complained that the people around him didn't care about him. Unsure of who he could trust, he had no safe place to go. He felt abandoned and depressed. And because he was being chased by Saul, he was exhausted and ready to faint. David eventually found a cave to hide out in with his army. David became keenly aware that God was his only refuge.

Most of us are not physically running from someone. But in our spirit, we may be fleeing from a number of things:

- the vengeance of others
- difficult work
- a painful past
- judgment from others
- our own insecurities

Do you need a refuge?

By definition, a refuge is a dwelling where people flee to get away from unsafe places or people. But we need more than a temporary fix. We need a long-term solution. We need a refuge that is within our reach at all times — faithful, and continual. That can only be God.

Psalm 46:1 tells us, *God is our refuge and strength, a very present help in trouble.* How fitting that Martin Luther's classic hymn, "A Mighty Fortress Is Our God," is based on Psalm 46.

God is our safe place — the One to whom we run — our only dependable source. Wiersbe said, "He doesn't protect us in order to pamper us. He shelters us so He can strengthen us to go back to life with its duties and dangers."[44]

We need to run to our cave — our private place — and into the presence of our Mighty Fortress. In this refuge we're able to attain rest, regain strength, and map out our next steps.

Make It Personal

Are you running from something today? If so, how would you describe the chase? Where is your cave — your private refuge?

Today I Bring Praise and Thanksgiving For

How Should We Pray?

Read Psalm 143

Key Verse: 143:1 *Hear my prayer, O Lord, give ear to my supplications.*

At age nine, I trusted Jesus to be my Savior. I knew many Bible stories but didn't understand much about theology, how to apply Scriptures, or how to pray. My prayers were logical for a child: "Jesus, please help me with _____." Years of spiritual growth taught me the importance of prayer. Additionally, I gained a more spiritually sophisticated vocabulary. But you know what? After more than forty-five years of prayer, I've returned to my childhood way of praying.

God is sovereign. He hears every sound in creation, including the childlike prayers we whisper at our kitchen tables. God knows our thoughts, so giving God information isn't the purpose of prayer. Prayer is communication. Through it, we establish and maintain a relationship with God. We communicate with Him to know Him more intimately. Fancy words aren't necessary; our natural vocabulary is sufficient. No pretense. Just be open and real with God.

An acronym that can assist us when we pray is this:

A Adoration. Tell God what you love about Him. Adoration includes praising God for His attributes — like His faithfulness, mercy, and kindness.

C Confession. Acknowledge sin so nothing hinders the conversation. Psalm 66:18 says, *If I regard wickedness in my heart, the Lord will not hear.* Psalm 51:10 is a good prayer for confession: *Create in me a clean heart, O God, and renew a steadfast spirit within me.*

T Thanksgiving. Expressing appreciation is being thankful for what God has done in general and for you personally. Thanksgiving and adoration are often done at the same time, in the same sentence.

S Supplication. Ask God for the things you need and want. James 4:2 tells us, *You do not have because you do not ask.* Ask God to teach you to pray His will — doing things the way He wants. Pray for physical health but pray for emotional and spiritual health too.

James 5:16 tells us, *The effective prayer of a righteous man can accomplish much.* Prayer is powerful. Let's pray like we believe this.

Make It Personal

When is the best time for you to pray? Is it scheduled, impulsive, or both? In what ways would you like your prayer life to be strengthened?

Today I Bring Praise and Thanksgiving For

The Polished Woman

Read Psalm 144

Key Verse: 144:12 *Our daughters may be as corner stones, polished after the similitude of a palace* (KJV).

*I*n our key verse, God used the word "polished" to describe a woman. Most Bible translations say corner pillars, or pillars, but the *King James Version* uses *corner stone*. Polished can be defined as "shiny, as a result of being rubbed; accomplished, skillful, and refined." In the Hebrew, the word translated polished means, "to cut with a chisel; to make smooth." Biblical scholars liken a polished woman to an ornamental column — or corner stone — of a palace, chiseled by a sculptor.[45]

The implication is inspiring. To God, a polished woman is:

- Strong. A palace column is weight-bearing, supportable, and dependable. Just as columns support the structure, polished women undergird and lift one another. Their God-given strength enables them to resist Satan's attempt to destroy their self-worth, purpose, and identity.

- Beautiful. A plain, wooden column can provide support but the sculptor chisels away rough wood to create something extraordinary. The column's beauty reflects the pride and skill of its maker. Our beauty reflects the skill of our Creator. We're made in the image of Christ; we're beautiful because He is beautiful. Our physical

293

appearance changes, but our inward virtues are our greatest ornaments.

- Wise. Just as a woman turns to God for strength, she also turns to God for help, especially when she's being "rubbed the wrong way." Seeking God's help is always a wise decision.

- Refined. When adversity comes and we're rubbed against the hard places, the refining process begins. This process is similar to how a goldsmith refines precious metal. The heat of adversities and pain bring impurities to the surface, where God can scrape them off.

- A corner stone, pillar, or column is the focal point of the foundation and is both essential and valuable. What an honor to have this most important position in the eyes of God. Women were designed by God with and for a purpose. Polished women provide a sure foundation for families, communities, and nations. They're influential, competent accomplished, and dignified.

Today, God chisels and burnishes — creating beautiful polished women.

Make It Personal

In what ways do you feel like a polished woman? Can you identify areas in which God is still chiseling and burnishing?

Today I Bring Praise and Thanksgiving For

Continuous Praise

Read Psalm 145

Key Verse: 145:21 *My mouth will speak the praise of the Lord, and all flesh will bless His holy name forever and ever.*

While visiting the Mukti Mission in India I became accustomed to hearing the heart-felt expression "Praise the Lord." I was both surprised and amazed at how natural and how often the words of praise rolled from their lips. Most of the Christians I met in India, didn't come from Christian families. Becoming a Christian there, meant giving up everything. To follow Jesus meant they were outcast by their own people.

When I met new people who were Christians, they'd shake my hand and say "praise the Lord" like we say "hello, how are you?" in the West. Their stories and testimonies began with, "praise the Lord, let me tell you what God has done." Many, many times each day they praised God for His greatness, compassion, mercy, and faithfulness.

They spoke continuously of God's mighty acts and gave glory to Him for His provision — the drinking well from which they got their water, the food grown in their fields, and the dairy cow. One woman told me about the birth of her son. The umbilical cord had been wrapped around his neck, "but by God's grace he is alive and in college today," she said.

The stories never stop. These Christians, walk, breathe, and live with God on their hearts and minds. They take seriously the command to remember the things God has done and to praise God without ceasing. Their endless praise must be a sweet sound to God's ears.

Among these Christians, I felt the presence of the Holy Spirit hovering over their mission and the nearby streets. I witnessed many prayers being answered. Could it be that putting on the garments of praise and thanksgiving each morning had done this?

May we become as wise and as faithful as my friends in India.

Make It Personal

How will you praise God today?

Today I Bring Praise and Thanksgiving For

Freedom in Forgiveness

Read Psalm 146

Key Verse: 146:7 *The Lord sets the prisoners free.*

Although Christ sets us free, sometimes we remain in bondage. By refusing to forgive others, we become a slave to sin. My friend shares her story:

> My husband's ex-wife, Carol, is a manipulator and troublemaker. After I married my husband, Carol phoned to say she wished my husband was dead. Carol told their daughter that her father hated her. Carol was full of vengeance. She slandered my family, inflicting stress that affected my health. She didn't deserve forgiveness. Then one day I read in the Bible, "Pray for your enemies." I knew the enemy to whom God was referring. I had prayed for my family, but never had I prayed for Carol. Desiring to be obedient, I prayed — halfheartedly at first, then my prayers grew more genuine. Weeks passed. My fear and anger turned to compassion. I was able to forgive her. Forgiveness wasn't easy but God empowered me. Finally, I was free.

Forgiving someone is difficult. But God knows that harboring unforgiveness poisons our body and soul:

- From a medical viewpoint, doctors at the Mayo Clinic report that forgiveness "can reap huge rewards for your health, lowering the risk of heart attack; improving cholesterol levels and sleep; and reducing pain, blood pressure, and levels of anxiety, depression and stress."[46]

Conversely, the surge of negative emotions associated with unforgiveness harms our bodies.

- *From a spiritual viewpoint, God loves us and wants to free us from the bondage that unforgiveness brings.* Matthew 6:14 tells us, *If you forgive others for their transgressions, your heavenly Father will also forgive you.* Additionally, in Ephesians 4:32 we see, *Forgive each other, just as God in Christ also has forgiven you. Jesus forgives and we want to be like Jesus.*

Christ sets us free from unforgiveness (Galatians 5:1), for it is the *Spirit of the Lord who enables us to forgive. And where the Spirit is, there is freedom* (2 Corinthians 3:17).

When we choose to forgive, we choose to loosen our chains and be free!

Make It Personal

In what ways do you feel in bondage? Is there anyone you need to forgive?

Today I Bring Praise and Thanksgiving For

Healing for the Brokenhearted

Read Psalm 147

Key Verse: 147:3 *He heals the brokenhearted and binds up their wounds.*

I once tried to open the back of a picture frame with a knife. The end result was a deep cut between my thumb and index finger . . . and a trip to the emergency room. The doctor stitched me up and I was home within a few hours, wishing I'd been more patient with that frame; if only I'd taken the right steps and sought the right tool.

Stitches serve an important purpose. They hold wounds together until the injury is healed.

The word *heal* in our key verse is the Hebrew word *rapha* and means "to repair and thoroughly make whole; to mend by stitching." The word *broken* in the Hebrew is *shabar* and means "to break into pieces." Broken-hearted in this context means "crushed or destroyed or torn."

Do you feel shattered emotionally? Is your heart crushed?

Psalm 34:18 tells us *the Lord is near to the brokenhearted and saves those who are crushed in spirit.* God is close when we're hurting and broken. But He does something more. He heals our hurts by stitching us back together. Unlike the stitches in my hand, what God is doing on the inside isn't visible. We can't actually see the healing that is happening within our heart and soul. But the Great Physician is sewing us back together piece by piece in His perfect timing.

The Hebrew term for "bind up" is *chabash*; it means to "wrap up our wounds or hurts." Can you picture God wrapping a bandage around your pain?

That is what He wants to do. God is willing to bind up the heart that is broken. Are we willing to let Him? Call out to God today. Let the healing begin.

Make It Personal

In what ways do you need to be stitched up today? How is time healing your hurts?

Today I Bring Praise and Thanksgiving For

After God's Own Heart

Read Psalm 148

Key Verse: 148:13 *Let them praise the name of the Lord, for His name alone is exalted; His glory is above earth and heaven.*

Reading and studying the psalms we have learned they address nearly every topic important to us: friendship, hope, fear, trust, anger, depression, suffering, strength, obedience, and so much more. But one of the most important topics was a call to action for many of us. David's habit of praise, worship, and thanksgiving emphasized the importance of these three things. Ironically, we praise the One who is worthy, yet we're the ones who receive the blessings.

Clearly articulated through the Psalms are reasons God is worthy of our praise. David, one of the writers of the psalms, is an example for us. He called out to God and wept. He became angry and weary. He vented and questioned. But he also loved, respected, and revered God. And although a king himself, he honored the One True King with outbursts of praise. He was a man who learned to enter the presence of God.

David was an intelligent man who knew how to command an army. But those character traits aren't what made him successful. He made mistakes and poor choices, but that didn't make him unsuccessful. What made David successful was his humble dependence on God for his strength, wisdom, and abilities.

Acts 13:22 tells us, *[God] raised up David to be their king, concerning whom He also testified and said, "I have found David the son of Jesse, a man after My heart, who will do all My will."*

In David's quest to understand the true character of God and his desire to please Him, he was branded with the perfect label — "man after My heart."

This is why we love the imperfect David. We see a part of ourselves in him. No matter our past, our ever-changing emotions, our disappointments, or our defeats, we want the same God who remained faithful to David to remain faithful to us. We long to approach the throne of Almighty God in the same way that David did — uninhibited, without reservation, and with a sincere heart full of genuine praise.

We, then, will become women after God's heart. Praise the Lord!

Make It Personal

Are you a woman after God's own heart? Would you like to be? What steps will you take to move in this direction? How would God describe you? How would you like Him to describe you?

Today I Bring Praise and Thanksgiving For

God Is Pleased

Read Psalm 149

Key Verse: 149:4 *The Lord takes pleasure in His people; he will beautify the afflicted ones with salvation.*

As we've journeyed through Psalms together, we've seen amazing sides of God — His lovingkindness, forgiveness, judgement, and faithfulness, to name a few. Today, our key verse reminds us that God takes pleasure in us, too.

When my daughters were young, they dressed up in clothes and costumes and danced around. Seeing their imagination unfold and listening to their continuous laughter made me happy. I often burst into laughter with them. Now, my granddaughter plays with the same dress-up clothes. Her theatrical productions ignite memories, prompting me to smile about the precious memories and laughing about the new ones.

What do you think God's face looks like when He's pleased with His people? Is He smiling? Does He laugh? Who are His people?

When this psalm was written, God's people were the Israelites. But John 1:12 states that all who receive Christ as Savior, are His people: *But as many as received Him, to them He gave the right to become children of God, even to those who believe in His name. God's people – saved people – bring Him pleasure.*

The Hebrew word translated "take pleasure" is *ratsah*, meaning that God delights, accepts, approves, and enjoys. Isaiah 62:5 tells us, *Your God will rejoice over you.* When God observes our actions, He may clap, laugh, or shed a happy tear. And sometimes God the Father may look over at Jesus, seated on His right, and rejoice with Him.

Job 8:21 tells us, *He fills our mouths with laughter.* When we're pleased, we laugh. And when God is pleased, He laughs too.

God is joyful and desires that we be joyful too. He created God–pleasing moments to make us laugh and to make life better. Paul E. McGhee, Ph.D., an expert in laughter therapy, writes, "Humor lightens your burdens, inspires hopes, connects you to others, and keeps you grounded, focused and alert."[47] Of course, it does. God says in Proverbs 17:22, *A joyful heart is good medicine.* Be pleased, laugh, smile, and enjoy life. God does.

Make It Personal

Describe a time you felt God was pleased. Did you and God laugh together?

Today I Bring Praise and Thanksgiving For

Praise the Lord Forever!

Read Psalm 150

Key Verse: 150:6 *Let everything that has breath praise the Lord. Praise the Lord!*

My daughter texted me about something that had occurred that morning. Her words were cause for celebration. I responded with PTL. She texted back, "PTL? That's clever, Mom."

For the first time, I realized that millennials may not use the expression, "Praise the Lord," or write the PTL acronym.

But that's how the incredible book of Psalms ends. Three life-changing words: Praise the Lord! Praising God changes us. Praise puts the focus on God, where it belongs. The exclamation mark used in the NASB shows us that these words are written with passion and enthusiasm. What an incredible finale!

We have every reason to praise God. In Isaiah 25:1 we read, *Lord, you are my God; I will exalt you and praise your name, for in perfect faithfulness you have done wonderful things, things planned long ago* (NIV).

Moses said to God in Deuteronomy 3:24, *O Lord God, You have begun to show Your servant Your greatness and Your strong hand; for what God is there in heaven or on earth who can do such works and mighty acts as Yours?*

Read the above verse again, but this time substitute your name in place of "Your servant."

He has done mighty works in your life. Become committed

to praising the Lord — with your spoken and written words. Maybe then our younger generations will pick up this life-changing habit and write "praise the Lord" — even text it.

Praising the Lord may be an excellent conclusion to the book of Psalms. But it isn't our conclusion. In fact, it's just the beginning. As believers in Christ Jesus, we'll be praising God for all of eternity. We have so much to look forward to. Can you imagine!

Make It Personal

How will you integrate praise into your regular routine?

Today I Bring Praise and Thanksgiving For

About the Author

Deborah Presnell, M.A.Ed., whose career has spanned more than three decades of teaching — from elementary school to higher education, where she trained future teachers — is a member of Gardner-Webb University's Gallery of Distinguished Alumni, a published author, national speaker, and Bible study teacher.

She is also a national spokesperson for Mukti Mission in India as she partners with Mukti Mission US to bring hope, healing, and life to women and children of India.

Debbie is called to inspire women and feels honored when God allows her the opportunity to share at women's events about His faithfulness. For the past twenty-five years, she has spoken at teacher conferences and universities where she shines the light on her favorite topic: "The Inspirational Classroom: A guide for teachers in all school environments." This will be the subject of an upcoming book.

Debbie's first book, *Shine! Radiating the Love of God — A Bible Study for Young Women in Middle School and High School*, is used in her popular Shine Camp. Her other books include *Shining Through the Psalms — A 150-Day Devotional Journey*, and *Shine On! — Biblical Principles for Radiant Living*. Her articles have been published in the *Divine Moments* series. She blogs and brings inspirational messages on her Facebook page: ShineEveryDayNC.

Debbie and her husband, Alan, have three adult children and one granddaughter. She enjoys camping, riding her bike, helping coach a girl's running team, and she loves both the mountains and the beach.

When she's not busy writing or speaking, she serves as a substitute teacher in her local schools. But her best day is Sunday when her entire family gathers for lunch.

Visit her website at www.debbiepresnell.com. Email her at debpres@yahoo.com for information about having her speak to your group.

Thank You!

Without people to support me, this book wouldn't have been written. But that's what God does — He puts a team around us to accomplish His purpose.

I want to thank my writer's critique group, Blue Ridge Writers. Your feedback and encouragement were invaluable. A special thank you to Yvonne and Joni for reading nearly every psalm devotion and helping me cut words and get to my point. You both are brilliant.

Prayer warriors are necessary in every part of life, and this is true in the writing world as well. These precious godly women consistently prayed for me — for words, wisdom, patience, endurance, and knowledge. They provided daily encouragement and support. It's my honor to call you my friends and have you on my team: Donna, Eleanor, Paula, Cindy, Carrie, Tammy, and Gloria. You're the wind beneath my wings. And Donna . . . I loved every single 4:00 A.M. text that said you were up and praying for me.

I have a special appreciation for Gloria and Cindy. They read every single devotion's Scripture references to confirm they were correct. That was no easy task, since I'm a writer who sometimes inverts numbers.

Thank you to my writing mentor — for believing in me for more than a decade, teaching me the art of writing, and taking precious time to work with me. Yvonne Lehman, I love you.

I couldn't have imagined being blessed with Denise Loock as my editor. Thank you for cleaning up my words and helping me write what I meant to say.

I am filled with gratitude and appreciation to my publisher, Terri Kalfas, a fellow servant of the Lord, and now my close friend. Terri, you understand the intention of my heart. Thank you for believing in me.

I also want to thank the approximately 300 members of my online Psalm-a-Day Bible study group who went through the writing of this book with me. We studied and learned together. Thank you for your faithfulness and for trusting me.

Mostly, thank You, God, for putting this psalm book on my heart. I had no intention of writing a devotional, but you had other plans. In Your wisdom and providence, You planted the seed that would slowly take root. And now, five years later, Your words are ready to be harvested. May this book be impactful and used for Your glory. I love You, Lord!

End Notes

1 *New King James Version Thomas Nelson Study Bible*, footnote on Psalm 4:3, 766.
2 Warren W. Wiersbe, *Be Worshipful*, David C. Cook, 2009, 42-44.
3 Ralph Waldo Emerson, *Nature and Selected Essays*. Penguin, 2003.
4 Wiersbe, *Be Worshipful*, 46.
5 Wiersbe, Ibid., 210.
6 http://av1611.com/kjbp/kjv-dictionary/fool.html
7 Wiersbe, *Be Worshipful*, 66.
8 John Piper. https://www.desiringgod.org-
9 https://www.intouch.org/read/magazine/daily-devotions/willing-to-wait-for-gods-way. (Charles Stanley, "In Touch Magazine.")
10 National Institute of Health (NIH). agingcare.com-Marlo Sollitto
11 John MacArthur. www.christianity.com/theology/why-are-you-supposed-to-seek-gods-forgiveness-if-he-has-already-justified-you-11556624.html
12 https://www.phrases.org.uk/meanings/sticks-and-stones-may-break-my-bones.html
13 http://www.finnleo.com/pages/health-and-wellness
14 Edward Shorter, Ph.D.; "Sad, Worthless, Hopeless?" Psychology Today. 12 June 2014, https://www.psychologytoday.com/us/blog/how-every-one-became-depressed/201406/sad-worthless-hopeless
15 https://www.biblestudytools.com/dictionary/hope/
16 Wierbe, *Be Worshipful*, 176
17 Wiersbe, Ibid., 178.
18 https://en.oxforddictionaries.com/definition/chaos and peace
19 https://www.biblegateway.com/resources/dictionary-of-bible-themes/4846-shadow
20 http://www.dictionary.com/browse/shadow
21 http://time.com/4389726/harris-poll-happiness-index-2016
22 http://www.apa.org/topics/divorce/
23 https://www.mckinleyirvin.com/Family-Law-Blog/2012/October/32-Shocking-Divorce-Statistics.aspx
24 https://www.helpguide.org/articles/sleep/insomnia-causes-and-cures.htm
25 Billy Graham, "My Answer." Chicago Tribune, Chicago Times-N.Y. News Syndicate.

26 https://dictionary.cambridge.org/dictionary/english/keep
27 https://www.cbsnews.com/news/many-americans-are-lonely-survey-finds/
28 http://mentalfloss.com/article/71964/7-scientific-benefits-helping-others
29 Joni Earekson Tada. *Diamonds in the Dust: 366 Sparkling Devotionals.* Zondervan, 1993.
30 https://www.crosswalk.com/faith/spiritual-life/inspiring-quotes/40-powerful-quotes-from-corrie-ten-boom.html
31 *The Free Dictionary.com.* Wisdom/knowledge
32 Warren W. Wiersbe. *Be Mature- Growing in Christ,* (Colorado Springs: David C. Cook, 2008), 11.
33 https://gracequotes.org/quote/if-you-lack-knowledge-go-to-school-if-you-lack-wis/
34 Wiersbe. *Be Exultant,* 90-91.
35 https://philosiblog.com/2015/09/03/the-only-thing-worse-than-being-blind-is-having-sight-but-no-vision/
36 Charles Swindoll. https://www.brainyquote.com/quotes/charles_r_swindoll_155779
37 Wiersbe, *Be Exultant,* 153.
38 Piper. https://www.desiringgod.org/articles/talking-to-your-tears
39 Charles Stanley. *In Touch Daily readings for Devoted Living,* May 2018, p. 23
40 Coffman, James Burton. "Commentary on Psalms 131:1". *Coffman Commentaries on the Old and New Testament.* https://www.studylight.org/commentaries/bcc/psalms-131.html. Abilene Christian University Press, Abilene, Texas, USA. 1983-1999.
41 Wiersbe, *Be Exultant,* 180.
42 https://www.biblestudytools.com/commentaries/matthew-henry-complete/psalms/136.html
43 https://www.npr.org/sections/krulwich/2012/09/17/161096233/which-is-greater-the-number-of-sand-grains-on-earth-or-stars-in-the-sky
44 Wiersbe, *Worshipful,* 171.
45 https://www.biblestudytools.com/commentaries/treasury-of-david/psalms-144-12.html
46 https://www.hopkinsmedicine.org/health/healthy_aging/healthy_connections/forgiveness-your-health-depends-on-it/Karen Swartz, M.D.
47 www.helpguide.org/articles/mental-health/laughter-is-the-best-medicine.htm

CPSIA information can be obtained
at www.ICGtesting.com
Printed in the USA
BVHW051913060320
574292BV00004B/8